TOWARDS THE
SENSITIVE
BUREAUCRACY

TOWARDS THE SENSITIVE BUREAUCRACY

CONSUMERS, WELFARE AND THE NEW PLURALISM

Edited by
Drew Clode
Christopher Parker
Stuart Etherington

Gower

Published by
Gower Publishing Company Limited
Gower House
Croft Road
Aldershot
Hants GU11 3HR
England

Gower Publishing Company
Old Post Road
Brookfield
Vermont 05036
USA

British Library Cataloguing in Publication Data

Towards the sensitive bureaucracy: consumers,
welfare and the new pluralism.
  1. Great Britain — Social policy
  I. Clode, Drew II. Parker, Chrisopher,
  1946– III. Etherington, Stuart
  361.6'1'0941 HN390

Library of Congress Cataloging-in-Publication Data

Towards the sensitive bureaucracy.

  Bibliography: p.
  1. Public welfare — Great Britain. 2. Poor as
consumers — Great Britain. 3. Great Britain — Social
policy. I. Clode, Drew, 1946–   . II. Parker,
Christopher, III. Etherington, Stuart, 1955–
HV245.T67 1986 361.6'0941 86–9890
ISBN 0-566-05009-9
ISBN 0-566-05010-2 Pbk

Printed and bound in Great Britain by
Biddles Ltd, Guildford and King's Lynn

Contents

Contributors

STUART ETHERINGTON is Director of a National Voluntary Agency concerned with mental health services. Previously he was an advisor on social policy to a professional association. He has an MA in Social Services Planning and writes widely on a range of social policy issues.

CHRIS PARKER is a Staff Officer for East Sussex County Council Social Services Department. He has experience both of line management and policy development. He has an MA from Essex University, and is a regular contributor to a range of social service publications.

DREW CLODE is Editor of *Social Services Insight* journal. He has wide experience of social services and health service journalism, and is a qualified teacher. He holds a degree in Philosophy from Leicester University.

WILLIAM BINGLEY is Legal Director of MIND and Chairman of the 'Advocacy Alliance'. He is a qualified lawyer and is actively concerned with issues of client rights.

NICK BOSANQUET is a Senior Research Fellow at the Centre for Health Economics at the University of York. He has written extensively on public expenditure issues and has a particular interest in health and social services for priority care groups.

KEVIN CAREY is Overseas Manager of the Royal Commonwealth Society of the Blind. Prior to this he was a journalist with the BBC specialising in political affairs. He is an executive member of the Tawney Society and a prospective parliamentary candidate for the SDP/Liberal Alliance.

DAVID CHALLIS has worked in social services departments in the North of England, mainly concerned with the problems of mental disorder. He is at present working at the Personal Social Services Research Unit, University of Kent.

TIM COOK has a long history of work in voluntary organisations. Until 1985 he was Director of Family Service Units. He now works for the City Parochial Trust. He chaired the NCVO Working Party on Clients Rights.

JOAN EVANS was the Project Organiser for the Liverpool Parent Governor Support Project. She is currently working in residential child care and has had extensive experience of youth and community work.

CHRIS HEGINBOTHAM is the National Director of MIND. Prior to this he was the Assistant Director of Housing in a London borough. He has written and spoken widely on issues relating to consumer involvement in services.

DAVID KING is the District General Manager for Exeter Health Authority.

NICHOLAS MURRAY is a staff writer on *Social Services Insight* and a contributor to the *New Statesman*. He is also on the executive committee of an inner city community action group.

DEBBIE OUNSTED is Director of Habinteg Housing Association. She worked previously as Area Manager for Circle 33 Housing Trust in North London, following six years at Islington Borough Council and the GLC.

JEF SMITH is the Director of Social Services for the London Borough of Ealing. He has written widely on personal social services issues and served on the NCVO Working Party on Clients' Rights.

ANN SOFER is a former SDP member of the Inner London Education Authority. She is a regular contributor to *The Times* and *Times Educational Supplement* and has written widely on education issues.

JUDY WILSON has worked as a community worker in Britain and Botswana. She is leader of the Nottingham Self-Help Team and does freelance writing and consultancy.

Foreword
Michael Young

The new, or not so very new, or not at all new, Right has so far failed to demonstrate how liberty can be enhanced within the welfare services. They wanted to do this; it is indeed an article of their faith that it should happen, and can only happen when the hands of those who created these services are lifted off them. These services are too important (so they might argue) to be left to any of the successors of William Beveridge. Only those who believe in liberty beyond equality can give a new tinge to services still clouded by a musty and old-fashioned egalitarianism.

They have had their chance, and I cannot think of a single really notable success, even in schools where there was so much trumpeting of the new rights to be accorded to parents. The successors have, on any broad view, been failures, demonstrating that the most the 'innovators' intend to do is enhance the liberty of those who can pay. This is not the same as favouring the rich, though they have been favoured. Marianne Rigge and I started the College of Health to uphold the rights of consumers even when they have to bear the vulnerability which sickness and disease brings to them. We have, for example, published a number of reports on hospital waiting lists. The saddest thing has not been the figures about the extraordinary length of waiting lists in some districts but the individuals who have written in to tell us of the pressure they were put under to 'go private' to get a hip replacement operation (say) done in a few weeks by the same consultant who said that in the NHS he would not be able to operate for three to four years. Pain has driven some unfortunate people – by no means wealthy – to dive deep into their remaining savings. Such examples do not stand alone, or come only from the health services.

And yet, the failure in practice does not for a moment mean that no attempts to introduce more libertarianism into the welfare services should be made. For the Right is not alone in its criticism of the state's part in the welfare state and of the unkindness of some of the people who have managed to dress themselves in the mantle of the state, in Gateshead or Manchester, or even Torquay. When dispensing money or services, they still manage to behave as though they have paid for them out of their own private pockets, not from the taxes of all the rest of us.

The successors to Beveridge therefore need to come out of the wood and show what the new welfare could be like without the New Right to direct it. This can only be done by hard thought and practical application. The merit of this book is that some of the successors to Beveridge have broached directly one of the most difficult problems facing the new democracy, and done so out of a great deal of practical knowledge.

MICHAEL YOUNG
Chairman of College of Health

Acknowledgements

The authors wish to acknowledge the assistance of Francis Burt for typing the manuscript and Shirley Greene for undertaking the correspondence relating to the production of the book.

1 Introduction: Consumerism and Welfare
Drew Clode, Chris Parker and Stuart Etherington

Consumerism has never needed much stimulus to flourish within what is less and less being described as the welfare state. The high-water mark of the dominance of public services by their producers was reached, and held, in the infamously recorded winter of discontent, 1978–79. But it was a high-water mark which coincided with the nadir of that attitude with which both consumers and producers had approached their services: paternalism. With the breakdown of the shared expectations that paternalistic modes of behaviour imposed on both client and worker/teacher and taught/doctor and patient culminating in 1979 with such a loss of confidence in the good faith of the suppliers of public welfare, consumerism seemed the only possible ideology left untried.

Its rise owed as much to the blind alleys of the 1970s as to any illumination the politics of the 1980s might have shed upon it. But throughout the years of the Thatcher ascendancy, one dominant theme has been continuously shown to have been captured by the New Right: freedom of choice. That concept has been used, and is still being used, to excoriate the defenders of large-scale spending on social welfare and allowed Norman Fowler, the then Secretary of State for Social Services, to tell directors of social services that freedom and consumer control are key features of the Conservatives' social policy and that state-dominated services deny people the opportunity to engage in real choices.

How far that ideological stance can be, or has been, translated into providing qualitatively better services remains still to be convincingly assessed, but there is no doubt that traditionally, the most common argument deployed against those who plan for a distribution of services according to need is that it removes the decision as to what services should be provided from consumers. Consumers cannot exercise choice by purchasing services, so key factors like the influence of demand on distributing services are taken away. There is no longer any clear link between the willingness of consumers to purchase services and the ability of suppliers to provide that service: the crucial fiscal link between supply and demand is broken when decisions are made to provide services according to some other criteria or rationing device.

Conservatives have attempted to reverse this trend and re-establish a link between service purchase and provision. The most notable way in which this has been developed in social services is in the subsidy now offered to private residential care homes – not competition in the strict sense of the word, in that direct subsidy is being paid for the provision of service. In fact it is a switch from state provision to state subsidy. There may be many reasons why this has happened. Some, including those in government, have argued that it was never a clear policy decision. Others may see it as an attempt to reduce the strength of public sector trade unions, lowering the unit cost of providing care in the short term and increasing productivity. The subsidy, however, has distorted the market. Consumers are free to purchase residential care in a variety of locations but are not provided with the same financial incentives to purchase domiciliary care or day care. If this subsidy was to represent an enhancement of consumer choice then it would need to be extended far beyond the boundaries of private residential care. It would then quickly expose the conflict between equality and liberty. The exercise of individual choice and individual purchasing power might mean that those with greater levels of resources could purchase a better quality of service. They could do this either in areas where there is no state subsidy offered or they could 'top up' their state subsidy with personal incomes to purchase a better standard of service.

Not only would personal social services be selective – a position to which they have always been condemned – but there would be no attempt to match needs with the resources available. Much the same argument could be extended to the service credit notion suggested by Bosanquet and to schemes in other service areas like education voucher systems. Discounting the administrative difficulties which these types of credit system involve they cannot ensure an equitable distribution unless the total amount that individuals are allowed to spend is capped at a certain point, or the additional service which could be purchased is minimised. Conflict between liberty and equality in the negative sense is no longer confined to textbooks but becomes the reality for consumers of residential care. And although we have chosen a recent example within the history of personal social services, any of those services with which we deal in this volume could be, or in a limited way, have been subjected to the same tensions and friction that the liberty/equality divide can produce. The knack of finding a social policy which maintains a balance between an individual's wealth, and an assessment of his or her educational, health, social or housing needs is persistently elusive, and we do not pretend to have found that balance. But many of the arguments in our opening sections address themselves directly either to ways of establishing such a balance, or the implications of failing to find it.

The second series of initiatives around consumerism are more concerned with organisations. Attempts to enable consumers to exercise some formal control over services by enabling them to sit on various advisory committees have often failed, although there are notable exceptions. The conflict here is between representative and participative democracy. It could be argued that in electing representatives through the formal political process consumers have made decisions locally and centrally about the policies which they wish to be adopted. Leaving aside the extent to which their local choice makes any sense in the light of central control over local spending, the argument also presents other problems. When voters vote they exercise their preferences in conglomerate forms. Parties themselves represent a coalition of views. Policies on personal social services for example are often not made explicit. But would attempts to formalise any democratic pluralism at a local level also run the risk of appearing undemocratic?

One consumer group achieving prominence may pursue its objectives in a way which less articulate groups are unable to do. Self-advocacy for one particular group may mean fewer resources for another. With many factions amongst social service consumers could there be any formal mechanism which might improve direct participation in decision-making?

Would the extension of the role of community health councils to personal social services really represent an extension of participative democracy?

Unfortunately, many of the more vocal voluntary organisations, who are alleged to be in a better position to represent consumers, are client group-focused, and some client groups are more popular than others, able to elicit greater public support. Perhaps one way forward might be found by those social services departments who are looking towards decentralisation as a way of encouraging participation. The more local the service the less likely that client-based voluntary groups will dominate proceedings. Building a natural constituency is very important. Parker (*Social Work Today*, 17.12.84) has argued that it might be possible to transpose school governor systems across to patch social service teams – a notion not without its problems. Is there a sufficient natural constituency, as in a school, to make this system work. Certain preconditions would certainly be required, and the extent to which budgetary control is decentralised would be crucial. The adding of a formal political dimension perhaps making ward councillors more directly involved in the provision of services might help and this could feature as a result of plans to decentralise social service departments in certain authorities. It is a trend worth watching. However, even this type of consumerism presents problems of equality. Not in this case in terms of purchasing power, but in the problems which decentralised services might face in maintaining territorial equality. One area, with articulate, probably middle-class groups, would undoubtedly be able to argue for greater levels of resources than those areas where people were less used to being given opportunities to control their lives. The result may be quite marked territorial inequalities not only between regions, but within local authorities. Yet linking participation to less formal structures like self-help groups may not solve the problem. Self-help initiatives might be more prominent in areas where people are more articulate, and territorial equalities would remain. There is plenty of case material which suggests that middle-class people are likely to be more articulate and aware of the formal political process than working-class people. Again, there may be compromise solutions for social services. An equalisation formula, similar perhaps to RAWP in the NHS, but with additions to represent demands on personal social services, might be applied to decide the overall distribution of resources between wards. Within those overall budgets, under a lower level of political control, decisions could be made by fora or by groups which involve consumers and non-consumers alike.

Neither, has there been any real work done on the exercise of formal civil, or less formal consumer rights on the one hand, and its impact on professional or trades unionist defensiveness. Any accretion to, say, parents of power within a school must necessarily mean a diminution of the power exercised by that school's teaching staff. Yet the implications of that have not in any way been taken on board by those educationists who have extolled the virtues of community education.

The third aspect of consumerism with which we are concerned operates on a much more individual level. It is perhaps a strange way of looking at consumerism to suggest that certain types of services might encourage consumer involvement by working out individual plans. Consumer involvement in problem-definition and in deciding on the way in which intervention will be structured is important. Access to files and other service information which may have some relation to decisions about the client's life cannot be seen as a separate area existing in a void because sharing information somehow appears to be a 'nice thing'. Information enables more informed choice. Apart from civil liberties issues relating to the correct recording of facts, it also enables the consumer to understand why decisions have been made and to become more active in deciding about what services they might require.

Running parallel to this, but still at an individual level, are the provision of advocacy services. These services have been most prominent in mental illness and mental handicap services although the recent changes in child care legislation and the appointment of independent guardian ad litems will lead to similar developments in this area of policy. If these trends are welcomed it might enable consumers to exercise greater power over professional judgements. Often the assertion of rights will need to be aided by advocates, but again this is no bad thing. There may however be a bad fit between rights and service provision. It is more easy to deploy rights arguments to resist services and treatment of a particular kind than to promote the provision of service. The history of UK legislation unlike that of the United States rarely establishes a right to service. There are numerous examples of the non-implementation of social legislation which has gone untested before the courts or when tested has been found to be wanting. There is undeniably a conflict between rights and services. The right to services is something which some organisations have tried to establish without avail but it is a course which might be pursued if we had more strengthened and more organised advocacy systems. Some developments are beginning in mental health with several advocacy projects being established in psychiatric hospitals. It may be that the extension of the rights approach to child care may be accompanied by similar developments in all the fields with which we are concerned.

Welfare services cannot exist in a vacuum divorced from ideas of liberty and equality. The approach which each of these two sets of ideas suggest are often at odds. Each can be traced through the three main strands of consumerism which we have considered in relation to personal social services. In fiscal-led consumerism the distinction between equality and liberty is clear. In organisation-led consumerism, the distinction, while being territorial, is none the less obvious. In individual-led consumerism the right to freedom needs to be balanced more keenly with the right to treatment.

In the pages that follow we have asked our authors to consider each of these aspects of consumerism as they have spilled out into all the main gulleys of British welfare provision. It will, perhaps, be a long time before the economics of our public services will ever again be so divorced from political realities as they might have seemed to have been in the immediate post-war decades. But there is no excuse, and we hope this volume makes it clear that there is no excuse, for using the politics of welfare provision to cloud and obfuscate the ideas that ought to underpin it.

DREW CLODE
CHRISTOPHER PARKER
STUART ETHERINGTON

Part I
Consumerism

Introduction

The welfare consensus which dominated the post-war years is no longer accepted without criticism. The days when politicians secured resources and professionals disposed of them is now surely over for ever. It is difficult to assess why this change has taken place. New libertarian philosophies first espoused by the New Right are beginning to find practical expression. Although espoused by the Right, these ideas have lessons too for the radical Left who are similarly rejecting purely municipal solutions.

The growth of consumerism represents one facet of this shift in values. It creates a challenge for policy-makers and practitioners alike, and it demands a new framework for understanding public welfare. Part I of this book attempts to meet this latter demand.

The essays in this section expand our Introduction, each considering in turn one aspect of consumerism. Chapters 3 and 4 represent a more radical picture, such is the nature of their subject. Each, starting from different positions, reaches a remarkably similar conclusion. Bosanquet (Chapter 3) documents the growth of multiple suppliers. He concentrates not only on freeing the demand side of welfare through the use of the social security system and vouchers but also ways in which supply side factors might also be influenced through multiple points of funding in housing, health and personal social services. Fiscal consumerism does not exist only in the realm of ideas and, as Bosanquet reminds us, many existing policies illustrate a tendency to open up welfare services via financial mechanisms. By concentrating on the mechanism of supply and demand, fiscal methods become slightly less ideologically rigid. Concentration on the demand mechanism tends to lead to liberal welfare services concentrating on individual decision-making. Switching to supply-side factors can encourage collective alternatives similar to those mentioned elsewhere in this volume.

Carey, however (chapter 4), tends away from collective solutions. He points out the fundamental antagonisms between the enjoyment of greater liberty and greater equality. The acquisition of rights implies an ability to make rational choices. This in turn leads him to consider the use of cash rather than 'in kind' transfers so beloved by welfare professionals. He does however concede that there may be areas where rights are not acquired – for example, child care, where services in kind might still be required. Welfare services do not only exist for those who want them. Some aspects of the welfare state are more closely concerned with social control. An extension of the rights thesis here would involve redress mechanisms similar to those in the penal or mental health systems.

Chapter 2 by Tim Cook is more directly related to reforming existing welfare services than with replacing them wholesale.

Given that professional and managerial power is likely to stay with us for some time, his is a timely chapter pointing both to the problems and prospects for consumer participation. Shifting the focus from individual rights in the strict sense to good practice within existing services, Cook details the advantages and disadvantages of participatory systems. One problem which will be of particular concern to readers interested in decentralised services is the inherent conflict between citizen and user. This may emerge as a serious problem with local control of many services, as it has in the past with housing provision.

New ideas take several years to become policy options. Policy options in turn take time to become services. We know what the old welfare system was like. It was centralised, bureaucratised and over-dominated by professional interest. New welfare services will need to move into uncharted waters. These three chapters are some of the first signposts to new destinations.

2 Participation
Tim Cook

In a Settlement House in South London lies a dusty annual report for the year 1897. In it reference is made to a coffee bar project to help young delinquents. The management of the scheme was characterised by the fact that the delinquent boys attending the coffee bar elected their own representatives to serve on the management committee. This is a salutary reminder of how long ago others trod the path that we now tread. It is an even more forceful reminder of how long it takes to persuade people of the wisdom of certain courses of action. There is now an ever-increasing interest in the involvement of consumers in the welfare organisations established to serve them. Yet it is equally clear that the interest and debate it has engendered has not been matched by practice. The aspirations seem to be there but the knowledge to translate them into action is lacking. Some would argue that the professional power-base is too strong ever really to let go (Wilding, 1982), or that to give consumers real control over the production of professional welfare services is in effect to challenge fundamentally the functions of the state in a capitalist society (Hoggett, 1985).

The confusion we are in when trying to progress in this area is most aptly illustrated in two ways.

First, we are never clear as to how we should even describe the consumers of the services. For social services in particular this is a problem when client, user, consumer, participant and member all jostle for recognition (National Council for Voluntary Organisations, 1984). In education, is it the parents or the pupils who are the consumers?

Second, unbridled consumerism is not even always what the consumers themselves want. Proposals that emerged tentatively in 1984 from the Department of Education and Science to give parents a majority on school governing bodies were rejected by representative parental organisations not least because that was not in their view the way to improve education, the underlying aim behind the original proposals.

More cynically it is surprising that just when resources are scarce, how ready local and central government are to propose greater consumer control be it by parents on school governing bodies or tenants in housing management arrangements.

It is relevant to make just a brief comment on self-help groups, an increasing phenomenon in the pattern of social and health service provision and to a much lesser extent in education. That consumers have felt the need to set up their own services reflects to some extent what they feel about their involvement in the mainstream services. But however powerful and rapid the growth of self-help, it is highly probable that a crucial and significant part of welfare services will always have to be provided through the more traditional or orthodox system whatever the nature of that particular partnership with other systems. This is likely to be the case if only because of the size of some of the problems being faced. It will also be likely because of the nature of some of the areas where services are needed. Self-help in some inner city areas clearly has its limitations (Knight and Hayes, 1981).

Whilst fully acknowledging the vitality and importance of the self-help developments, it is perhaps worth entering a few caveats. Consumers could find themselves as representatives participating in the operation and management of main services as well as being in self-help groups: a dual role that could be both uncomfortable and divisive. For self-help can arise as a force in opposition to and as an expression of disenchantment with the traditional welfare services. Equally, self-help groups may not necessarily see themselves as having a function of providing and delivering services, except of course in so far as a group is itself a service to its members.

Until recently self-help groups have not been subject to very detailed study. In the United Kingdom one survey (Richardson and Goodwin, 1983) provides a valuable and realistic analysis of self-help organisations in practice. The authors point out the very positive effects of the groups but also highlight the difficulties. For example one of the most common themes to emerge from every organisation and virtually every group studied was 'the apathy of the membership, their lack of willingness to put themselves out to help run their group'. The virtual failure of claimants' unions to make any major impact on social security services or even to sustain themselves as an effective critical movement may equally well demonstrate the limitations, for whatever reasons, of self-help and allied developments.

If we are to talk of consumerism in welfare organisations it is necessary to be clear as to how we use the term. If it is to have any meaning at all it must, I would argue, contain the notion of participation in the decisions affecting the consumers.

Brager and Specht (1973) define participation as follows: 'Participation refers to the means by which people who are not elected or appointed officials of agency and of government, influence decisions about the programme and the policies which affect their lives.' At whatever level, it is the consumer participation in the decision-making process that should be the focus. Merely to say that consumers influence decisions is insufficient. After all, clients could be said to have *influence* if an authority took notice of a user opinion survey. Necessary though the latter may be at times, it is not a substitute for participation. Indeed, it can be misused to give a false legitimacy and authority to decisions which others then claim have user sanction. Sadly even this limited degree of user influence is very undeveloped (Smith, 1985).

There are a number of points that should be made to reinforce the importance of the notion of participation:

1. Participation should not be viewed as an optional extra for a service but as an essential part of it (Rose, 1970);
2. Participation is a means to an end not an end in itself. Participation, for example, cannot and should not of itself be used to make good any deficiency in services or to provide a gloss for services which are under-resourced;
3. Participation should be a feature at every stage of the services. Some have argued that it should occur at four distinct levels: strategic planning, the planning of service provision, delivery of services and feedback (Deakin and Willmott, 1979). Participation clearly has to be more than involvement in decisions about where old people's homes are to be located or what names are to be given to the homes;
4. Participation is not socio-therapy or market research but is eventually about the issue of power (Graycar, 1977). And although it is about power, the mistake should not be made of then equating participation with power equalisation. It is, in fact, possible for the reverse to happen because of the expertise of superiors who can strongly influence subordinates and lay members (Hulder and Wilke, 1970). This needs to be recognised because efforts made to distinguish expert knowledge, which is viewed as acceptable, from expert power which is not, do not seem to recognise that in many situations the knowledge is itself the power. Parent governors on school governing bodies, for example, can have an important contribution to make. But just as easily they can reinforce the authority and power of the head of the school because of a natural lay deference to the expert who is in charge.

In summary then, participation occurs when consumers are provided with the opportunity to contribute to and share in the decisions that affect the lives of the consumer groups they represent. This should occur within organisational structures that they can understand and use. The consumers then become another group within the decision-making processes. There are no assumptions made that they are the most important group; but their presence is essential.

Over some years now we have been accustomed to reading occasional accounts of consumer participation in the management of services provided for them. However, it is the apparent inability to make significant advances either in quantity or quality that is so striking. Jewell (1973) described self-management in local authority day centres. Carter (1981) was later able to describe other examples, but by no means could consumerism in local authority day centres be said to be embraced willingly and universally by the policy-makers, professionals and politicians alike. The same relatively slow progress can be noted too in housing. Derricourt (1973) writes guardedly of the problems and hopes of tenant involvement in housing management. Savill (1982) writes rather more optimistically of the potential impact on and benefit for tenants as a result of the Housing Act 1980, and the management rights given to tenants. But increasingly for tenants it has become essential to have some control over local budgets if consumers' involvement is to have any meaning at all (Gregory, 1985).

Local consultative groups involving users of social security offices was recommended by the National Consumer Council in 1977 and a report produced by the Department of Health and Social Security (1978) which in turn recommended a feasibility study in two areas. Nothing came of this and, as Richardson (1983) says, 'the idea has not arisen since on any political agenda', despite the crisis facing supplementary benefit offices which have culminated in strikes in some areas (Ward, 1985). Some slight inroads are made in the health services with the emergence of patient participation in some general practices (Royal College of General Practitioners, 1981) but again only the surface is being scratched. The Taylor Report (Department of Education and Science, 1977), with its strong push for more parental partnership in the running of schools, has still not produced the impact many hoped for. The Education Act 1981 made parent governors a requirement for schools (it is astonishing to think that was necessary and not a universal practice by then). The Barclay Report's recommendation to set up local welfare advisory committees (National Institute of Social Work, 1983) would have given consumers some say in service planning and delivery. The idea has met with very strong resistance from many including the Association of Directors of Social Services.

All these delays, difficulties and obstructions are less easy to explain when modest attempts to give consumers a greater say in services are invariably so successful – at least in contrast to the fears and anxieties beforehand. Skinner (1980), Cranwell (1982), Edwards (1983), Flower (1983), Stainton (1984) and Zipfel (1984) have all described modest experiments in social services, housing and education where consumers have been involved effectively to the benefit of all concerned.

What then prevents a much more accepted and rapid development of consumer involvement in the welfare services? In an attempt to answer this key question, I want to look in detail at the problems for consumers in the personal social services.

We should recognise that the people termed 'clients' and who some now feel should participate in and have some responsibility for the services, have in fact been created clients by those self-same services. The predominantly passive role that has been the state of clienthood will not be reversed overnight. Of course, clients should be involved in decisions that affect their lives, but the paradox is that for a long time we have been telling them that they are not capable of that. Indeed, some clients may well feel that services could be worsened by having 'people like them' participate in the services.

We also have to be very careful about how we use the term 'client'. If used too glibly there is the imminent danger of making the assumption that anyone can represent anyone else. Clienthood, in other words, is itself seen as a common enough denominator to allow such cross-representation. We may well say such a position is self-evidently not true. But it is surprising to note how often divisions and conflicts within groupings quickly come to the fore inhibiting participation and highlighting the heterogeneity of the term client. In one study (Richardson and Goodwin, 1983) of self-help groups, the authors found, for example, that young parents of mentally handicapped children 'could feel little sense of kinship' with the elderly parents and would not join the groups. Lone parents too were often divided by a range of ages and mixed social backgrounds. One English local authority rejected a committee of blind people as not representing the blind client group as most blind people, they argued, were over 70 and 'they do not join organisations' (Low *et al.*, 1979).

There may therefore need to be more recognition of the considerable differences of opinion and policy disagreements amongst clients themselves. For example, Kramer (1981) found that 'in England the younger more articulate spokesman or the physically handicapped, especially among those who have not been disabled from birth, strongly oppose efforts to improve institutional care and concentrated instead on improving community services. Older persons and others less able to function in the community are much less articulate.'

Some experience suggests (Liffman, 1978) that clients may not easily be able to work from their own individual experiences. This would suggest therefore that clients, initially at least, are much more satisfactorily engaged in participatory models at a very local level. Here the argument would be at one with advocates of decentralisation. Wood (1985), for example, has described Sheffield's pilot neighbourhood fora which have the power to put resolutions direct to service committees and are able to call for reports. However the fora are based on areas covering 10,000–15,000 people and it might be argued that these are still too large a base to give a sense of involvement, even via representatives, to many service users.

Real client participation must also raise a question as to how far this fits in and is compatible with the democratic processes whereby councillors see themselves as elected to carry out policies for which they believe they have a public mandate. There is a conflict between client representation and the normal democratic processes and reconciling the 'local government machine to the eccentricities of the neighbourhood' (Cummins, 1984). This is further highlighted when local councillors have become career politicians whose 'links with the electorate have sometimes become more fragile' (Smith, 1985).

If clients do participate in the system, how do they retain the value and freshness of the client perspective and avoid being seduced into becoming part and parcel of the system? This then requires us to address the problems of the structure within which clients are invited to participate.

There is at the centre of the consumerism debate a fundamental issue namely that any client participation in the management and operation of social services is in fact participation in a model that has already been determined by those in authority, and into which clients are now invited. There may always therefore be the prior problem of how to enable clients or others to engage in the discussion about the nature of the participative management model in which they will have a voice. This is a critical issue, as failure to engage clients in participation will almost certainly mean that 'we' conclude 'they' are not interested rather than asking ourselves whether the model is the appropriate one. In the wider area of public planning there is little doubt that the failure to engage significantly the public in the participation process leaves planners to view the public as 'apathetic'. They do not seem to examine the processes in which they have asked the public to participate.

It is not only the structure that is too often predetermined but also the language used to make the structure function. It is certainly a language unfamiliar to clients. Smith (1985) has suggested that for consumers to be involved in local government community work, skills may be needed to occupy the middle ground between council and community if effective communication is to exist between the two. Tyne (1978) found in his study of mentally handicapped people that 'many groups found their dealings with the formal systems of representations to be deeply frustrating'. In view of this it may well be that formal consumer participatory mechanisms do not in fact ensure that the decisions accurately affect consumer preferences. Indeed, the British Association of Social Workers (1980) has suggested that 'because social work clients are particularly disadvantaged and stigmatised in society, that special arrangements for their participation in policy-making should be made outside the conventional political structure'. An important critique (Wilding, 1982) of professional power has argued strongly for a partnership between professionals and clients in which '*ad hoc* representative institutions will need to be established for there are "no slick institutional solutions"'.

It is of great interest, therefore, to watch the emergence of new structures that offer at least some scope for more relevant client participation. In England, Liverpool is attempting to establish a community welfare council and another authority has established a social care assembly. These are new structures and while not aiming solely to bring about client participation, they may well·be the first essential practical steps.

But perhaps the greatest dilemma of all is that whatever the service consumer involvement is, is partly a value statement that may well be at variance with other values. Graycar (1977) summarised this problem when he argued that the values of participation, leadership and expertise exist in a dialectical relationship and that social justice and the effectiveness of programmes would be limited if too much reliance is placed on one value alone.

All these problems were identified as particular to 'clients' in the social services. But they are equally echoed in other services. Warnock (1985) is suspicious of parental participation in schools as only the 'pushy' parents come forward, i.e. they are unrepresentative. Derricourt (1973) found a 'marked disparity between leadership styles of poor working-class people, and the ideal democratic behaviour which they are expected to adopt on local authority committees'. Representative local people then have to adopt the style of the committee and 'become unable to represent the people he is supposed to be representing'.

Boaden and colleagues (1982, p. 179) conclude a study on public participation in local services:

> In planning, transportation, the health service and education, we find it is middle-class individuals and middle-class organisations who become involved on the majority of occasions. Even in those services where benefits are more likely to go to working-class recipients, such as social services and housing, the individualistic client approach of the professionals involved, and the mode of service delivery, inhibits a class-based participation, as the difficulties of claimants' unions and tenants' associations amply demonstrate.

Richardson (1983), p. 128) poses the most acute dilemma of all.

> It is argued that tenants or patients or workers should be able to have their say, but what is really wanted is that they should put into practice certain policies or be helped to come round to a particular point of view. But what happens when the results go the 'wrong way'? How many advocates of a participatory process will cling tenaciously to this position when they find its effects not to their liking? Some will and some will not, it is a difficult decision, involving a conflict – and therefore some trade-off – of basic values'.

A good example of this would seem to be in the Liverpool Council Race Relations Committee which had coopted twelve members of the Liverpool black caucus as representatives of the black community in Liverpool. However the black caucus members objected to the committee's appointment of a particular race relations officer. As Williams (1985) wrote 'by disagreeing the caucus quickly became "unrepresentative" and was condemned as such . . .'.

This problem of trade-off is especially acute when we put alongside consumerism the value of 'citizen power'. Consumer participation in services and citizen participation in service planning can be at total variance. Deakin and Willmott (1979) have even suggested 'citizen power' could worsen social services. Local community campaigns to prevent the establishment of facilities for vagrants or the mentally ill illustrate this (Cook and Braithwaite, 1978). A German study commented: 'A public interest in fighting against motorways or nuclear power stations is far more welcome than their interest in improving the conditions of the underprivileged' (International Council in Social Welfare, 1974).

It has always seemed to me that the interest in decentralised services, especially in housing and social services, that has emerged so strongly in the 1980s, ought to present the best opportunity to bridge the gap between consumer interest and citizen power. It surely ought to be the case that the more locally-based the services the more accessible, visible and comprehensible they should be to *all* in the vicinity.

The numerous accounts to date of the 'going local' movement have sadly not so far indicated whether that is the case (Hadley and McGrath, 1980, 1985; Hadley and Hatch, 1981; Hadley *et al.*, 1984). What has been much clearer from the 'going local' developments is that it is primarily seen as a better and potentially more effective method of providing a service which for the professionals involved just makes better sense. The notion of consumer involvement has become diluted in rather more esoteric debates between the professionals. As Croft and Beresford (1984) have consistently pointed out, the decentralisation structures are ironically not noted for their attempts to consult or involve consumers in the changes being made. Not all local politicians view decentralised services as warmly as some professionals as they can see their own power-base and access to resources being diluted and shared. It still remains unclear whether 'going local' is a rallying cry or a serious policy initiative that will be sustained and strengthened to bring it closer to Croft and Beresford's vision of community control which some would argue is its logical resting place.

Consumerism is one way of addressing growing concern about the effectiveness of many of the public services to which Hill (1984) and others have rightly drawn our attention. The forms in which consumer involvement in the services can take are in practice many and varied.

New steps will be needed first if consumers are even to begin to influence the services. The NCVO Report (1984) examined in some detail the wider questions of 'clients' rights' in relation to voluntary organisations in personal services. The evidence is not good that the self-proclaimed flexible and innovative voluntary bodies are attuned to consumer needs and aspirations. Clearly all services must address very basic matters affecting their consumers; readable literature about the service (in several languages), decent reception facilities, complaints procedures, agency statements on consumers' rights, and many more particular to the service in question.

Even if we embrace most fervently consumerism in the welfare services it would be unwise not to ponder some of the more immediate implications. These are too readily left unspoken or relegated to a secondary consideration. But the strong union opposition to social security advisory panels with user representation should be a reminder of the need to think through implications more clearly (Richardson, 1983).

First, it must be underlined that developments of consumer participation must take on board as a corollary staff participation in management (Brenton, 1978). There can surely be little long-term hope for consumer participation if the workers in the service have no say in the processes of management. At whatever level consumers are seeking to participate there would certainly be implications for the staff who are or have been directly working with them. There may be, for example, new training requirements which need considering. I do sometimes wonder whether the failure to move quickly in the area of consumer participation is due less to management's conservatism than to the staff's inability to respond when their traditional training base is no longer such a safeguard or protection for them.

It should not be imagined that the attempts to carry out policies of consumer participation can be affected without some resource implication. That has certainly been the experience of the physical planners when resource demands are made even when participation is little more than public relations and information-sharing. How many more resources might be needed in a major services context especially when we consider the persuasive arguments in favour of establishing quite new structures.

Finally, even when participation has been achieved it could lead to a situation of what Myrdal (1958) called 'created harmony' which then has the effect of diminishing the general impulse to such involvement. It may be, therefore, that pressures for participation go in cycles and need constant renewal.

There is one issue above all others that perhaps most readily encapsulates the tensions and dilemmas touched on in this chapter: that is racism. Virtually all the literature on consumerism or public participation makes little or no reference to racism nor to the racial differences in consumer groups. Racial harassment on housing estates has in 1984 and 1985 become a subject of public concern. The institutional racism of white-dominated public services has rarely been far from the public arena. The Swann Report (1985) and its controversial history showed in the field of education how tense and complex the issues in fact are. It should not require much imagination to see how even more complex consumer participation becomes when racism has rightly to be added to the equation. The apparent silence on the subject in the debate is itself an indication of just how uncertain we all are. Yet there is anecdotal evidence to suggest that in some services it is the thrusting, high-profile demands of ethnic minority consumers to be taken into consideration that has brought some services into a sharp realisation that in effect no group of consumers has really ever been considered when plans and policies are being devised.

While no one should minimise the problems involved, no examples come readily to mind of consumer participation at whatever level being eventually other than constructive and productive. The hopes and aspirations always seem to overcome the fears and anxieties.

We need to increase consumer participation because only in so doing will we acquire sufficient knowledge as to what needs to be done to make it work. We still know remarkably little about the processes involved and how far we have to change and how far consumers are engaged in the process have to change.

Professionals generally seem to be increasingly under attack in what has been called a guerilla warfare against the professions (Wilding, 1982). Some of the newer professions such as social work are particularly vulnerable, though teachers might justifiably argue that the age of their profession is no protection. Whatever the justifications for such attacks there seems little doubt that unless a much more active partnership is sought with consumers, that which is necessary and valuable within a professional service will be lost along with that which undoubtedly has been destructive or even repressive. It could be said that the professionals and the consumers both need each other to ensure the best development of services in the future.

It is just as possible for consumers to participate by coming together against something as it is for them to participate in it. There is traditionally a we/they dichotomy with the 'we' historically in the ascendancy. If participation is not treated seriously enough to help bridge the we/they divide, we may simply witness its perpetuation but with the 'they' in the ascendancy. Given the size and complexity of the social problems facing us that would seem to be of limited value in contrast to what genuine participation might well achieve.

At an individual level a user's participation in the service processes often enhances self-respect. Engagement in the organisational and management levels should have the same effect. But it will only occur if those of us who can influence policies and practices ensure that it happens. If consumer participation is pressed upon a reluctant management by the force of populist pressures then consumers involved in it could too easily be deskilled and experience a subsequent reduction in self-respect. We need to work for an increase in consumer participation so that it occurs in a way that enriches all of us rather than management seeing it as 'having to give in to them'. This very much seems to have been the attitude of one English local authority (Low *et al.*, 1979) where a consultative committee for the handicapped was restricted to being a vehicle for communication and information, and denied a role in contributing to planning and policy formation.

An increase is urgent if there is to be any chance of reaching and engaging client groups from within the ethnic minorities. This is now a pressing issue. It would be my view that without effective consumer participation it will be virtually impossible to understand the needs, let alone meet them, of, for example, many of the ethnic minority communities.

Too much has been learnt and developed from the limited participation we have had to date as well as from other movements like the self-help groups to believe that the main forms of direct welfare services can remain as they are.

Finally, it is vital that consumer participation in welfare services is seen to be operating and workable. The fear otherwise could be that participation is seen as fine for the educated and the articulate but not for the traditional welfare beneficiary. In that way a serious commitment to consumer participation in the welfare services may play a small but important part in altering society's perceptions about groups of people it might prefer to stereotype or to forget altogether.

In summary, it is crucial to work with and harness the tide of consumerism and not to stand against it.

Let me conclude on a cautionary note. We should always spell out for ourselves and for others exactly what we mean by consumer participation if we wish to pursue it as a policy. We should recall the American anti-poverty programme of the 1960s which had built into it as part of the legislation for the programme the concept of 'maximum feasible participation'. But the goal was never realised and the programme ended in what one critic (Moyniham, 1969) called 'maximum feasible misunderstanding'. A sad illustration of that misunderstanding can be found in the comments of a young lawyer involved in setting up the programme who said afterwards:

> I had never really conceived that participation would mean control by the poor of the community action. I expected that the poor would be represented something in the order of 15% to 25% of the board. Moreover, *I don't think it ever occurred to me or to many others that the representatives of the poor must necessarily be poor themselves.* (Moyniham, 1969; emphasis added)

References

Boaden, N. *et al.*, *Public Participation in Local Services*, Longman, London, 1982.

Brager, G. and Specht, H., *Community Organising*, Columbia University Press, 1973.

Brenton, M., Worker Participation and the Social Service Agency', *British Journal of Social Work* 8(3) (1978), pp. 289–300.

British Association of Social Workers, *Clients are Fellow-Citizens*, BASW, 1980.

Carter J., *Day Services for Adults*, Allen and Unwin, London, 1981.

Cranwell, K., 'One Monkey don't Make No Show', in P. Henderson *et al.*, *Successes and Struggles on Council Estates*, Association of Community Workers, London, 1982.

Cook, T. and Braithwaite, G., 'A Problem for Whom?', in T. Cook (ed.), *Vagrancy: Some New Perspectives*, Academic Press, London, 1979.

Croft, S. and Beresford, P., 'Patch and Participation: The Case for Citizen Research', *Social Work Today*, 17 September 1984, pp. 18–24.

Cummins, A., 'Calling Social Services to Account', *Community Care*, 6 December 1984, pp. 23–5.

Deakin, R. and Willmott, P., *Participation in Social Services: An Exploratory Study*, Personal Social Services Council, London, 1979.

Department of Education and Science, *A New Partnership for our Schools*, HMSO, London, 1977.

Department of Health and Social Security, *Social Security Users – Local Consultative Groups*, HMSO, London, 1978.

Derricourt, N., 'Tenants and Housing Management', in S. Hatch, *Towards Participation in Local Services*, Fabian Tract 419, Fabian Society, London, 1973.

Edwards, K., 'Don't Exclude Them from Responsibility', *Community Care*, 9 June 1983.

Flower, J., 'Creating a Forum', *Community Care*, 21 April 1983.

Graycar, A., 'The Relevance of Community Involvement to Social Welfare and Public Administration', *Australian Journal of Public Administration* 36(3) (1977), pp. 238–48.

Gregory, S., 'Endangered Estates', *Community Care*, 18 April 1985, no. 559, pp. 34–46.

Hadley, R. and Hatch, S., *Social Welfare and the Future of the State*, Allen and Unwin, London, 1981.

Hadley, R. and McGrath, M., *Going Local*, NCVO Occasional Paper 1, Bedford Square Press, London, 1980.

Hadley, R. and McGrath, M., *When Social Services are Local: The Normanton Experience*, Allen & Unwin, London, 1985.

Hadley, R. *et al.*, *Decentralising Social Services – A Model for Change*, Bedford Square Press, London, 1984.

Hill, M., *Better Services in Public Services*, Address to Family Service Units/Royal Institute of Public Administration Conference, 30 March 1984.

Hoggett, P., 'Decentralisation, Labourism and the Professionalised Welfare State Apparatus', in *The Politics of Decentralisation: Theory and Practice of a Radical Local Government Initiative*, eds Hoggett, P. and Hambleton, R. Working Paper 46, SAUS Publications, 1984.

Hulder, M. and Wilke, H., 'Participation and Power Equalisation', *Organisational Behaviour and Human Performance*, 5 (1970), pp. 430–48.

International Council in Social Welfare: German Executive Committee, Frankfurt, Development and Active Participation – Practicable Conclusions for the Social Services, *XVII International Conference of the International Council in Social Welfare*, Nairobi, Kenya, 1974.

Jewell, P., 'Self-Management in Day Centres', in S. Hatch, *Towards Participation in Local Services*, Fabian Tract 419, Fabian Society, London, 1973.

Knight, B. and Hayes, R., *Self-Help in the Inner City*, London Voluntary Service Council, 1981.

Kramer, R.M., *Voluntary Agencies in the Welfare State*, University of California Press, London, 1981.

Liffman, M., *Power for the Poor*, Allen & Unwin, London, 1978.

Low, C., Rose, G. and Cranshaw, B., *Participation in Services for the Handicapped: Two Contrasting Models*, Personal Social Services Council, London, 1979.

Moyniham, D.P., *Maximum Feasible Misunderstanding*, Collier-Macmillan, London, 1969.

Myrdal, G., 'The Quest for Democratic Participation', *Storr Lectures*, Yale Law School, 1958.

National Council for Voluntary Organisations, *Clients' Rights*, Bedford Square Press, 1984.

National Institute of Social Work, *Social Workers: Their Role and Tasks*, Bedford Square Press, London, 1983.

Richardson, A., *Participation*, Routledge & Kegan Paul, London, 1983.

Richardson, A. and Goodwin, M., *Self-Help and Social Care: Mutual Aid Organisations in Practice*, Policy Studies Institute, London, 1983.

Rose, H., 'Participation: The Icing on the Welfare Cake', in K. Jones and S. Baldwin (eds), *Yearbook of Social Policy in Britain 1975*, Routledge & Kegan Paul, London, 1976.

The Royal College of General Practitioners, *Patient Participation in General Practice*, Occasional Paper 17, London, 1981.

Savill, D., 'Council Tenants and the 1980 Housing Act', in P. Henderson *et al.*, *Successes and Struggles on Council Estates*, Association of Community Workers, London, 1982.

Skinner, P., 'Our Experience in Involving Children in Reviews', *Social Work Service No. 22*, Department of Health and Social Security, London, 1980.

Smith, J., *Public Involvement in Local Government*, Community Projects, Foundation, 1985.

Stainton, R., 'First Steps in Politics', *Teaching London Kids* No. 20, London, 1983.

Swann, Lord, *Education for All*, The Report of the Committee of Inquiry into the Education of Children from Ethnic Minority Groups, Cmnd. 9453, HMSO, London, 1985.

Tyne, A., *Participation by Families of Mentally Handicapped People in Policy-Making and Planning*, Personal Social Services Council, London, 1978.

Ward, S., *DHSS in Crisis: Social Security – Under Pressure and Under Review*, Child Poverty Action Group, London, 1985.

Warnock, M., *The Dimbleby Lecture*, BBC, 1985.

Wilding, P., *Professional Power and Social Welfare*, Routledge & Kegan Paul, London, 1982.

Williams, I., 'Militant Blunders On', *New Statesman*, 7 June 1985.

Wood, P., 'A Critical Tension', *Community Care*, 18 April 1985, pp. 36–7.

Zipfel, T., 'Tenants' Key Role in Improvement Schemes', *Peptalk*, No. 1, December 1984, Priority Estates Project, London.

3 Buying Care
Nick Bosanquet

The old pattern of public service used to be about services entirely tax-financed and publicly provided by people who are public sector employees with lifetime tenure. There has been no one great public pronouncement but pressures at the point of decision have moved services away from this model in a number of different fields. (Ritchie, *et al.* 1983)

— A 16 year old school leaver takes up a YTS place.
— A social services department finds a fostering placement for an older child.
— A woman of 79 uses a social security allowance to pay for a place in a private nursing home.
— A mentally handicapped client who has been in a hospital for a long time finds a place in a group home where the housing has been organised by a Housing Association and living costs are paid for out of supplementary benefit.

In all these cases tax money is being used in new and different ways; the mix of fiscal methods has changed.

On the demand side the old debate used to be about giving help in 'cash' as against help in 'kind'. In the first option there would be transfers which would raise people's income and purchasing power. They would then have more choice since they could decide to spend the money according to preference. Alternatively, they would be able to obtain a particular service which would be free at the point of consumption. On the demand side cash has become a more attractive option. It is possible to give people cash payments for more precise reasons to meet particular needs as with the attendance allowance and the mobility allowance. The idea used to be that help in cash involved a general uplift in income which could not be targeted at those in most need. The development of these new types of cash payment has shown that this is not necessarily so. The old argument that help in kind was much more selective is not so strong. There has also been increased use of what are in effect voucher systems within the public sector – that is, entitlements to pay for particular kinds of services. Thus a 16 year old has in effect a voucher which he can cash in for a YTS place: use for a place in a college of further education: or use to stay on at school. The new social security allowances are in effect vouchers which old people can try to cash in for a place in a residential home. There may be drawbacks to this, but their choice is certainly wider than if they had to rely on one monopoly public supplier.

On the supply side there has also been a widening of the options. There are many ways other than by direct public monopoly that the state can influence the pattern of supply. It could give subsidies to existing firms to alter their pattern of supply. It could assist voluntary organisations such as housing associations to increase supply; or it could work through local and central government. Thus there can be different fiscal means of giving help. The evidence suggests that the supply response to these new incentives can be very favourable. For example, in services for mentally handicapped people and for the mentally ill the combination of incentives operating in these services led to the creation of some 5000 places in group homes and small hostels in the course of the 1970s.

Looking at the various programmes, the current range of alternatives could be summarised as follows:

— To increase income support through general payments such as the pension, or child benefit.
— To increase support to people with particular needs for services but without any public initiative in supply. Examples of this are the attendance allowance, the mobility allowance and the social security allowance for residential care.
— To subsidise private suppliers to produce certain outputs for clients as a sideline to their main business as with the training places provided under YTS.
— To finance the development of new private and voluntary suppliers as with housing associations.
— To provide services through direct public employment but on fixed term contracts. Most new development in higher education for example are on fixed term contracts.
— To provide services through public initiative on the old model.

Is there any way of ranking these various methods? Or is choice likely to be a chance outcome of gut reaction and the local political balance? There are now some considerations which tilt the argument much more strongly both against public monopoly and against the supply of services without prices.

First, real choice for clients must involve the possibility of choosing between different suppliers. Secondly, a variety of suppliers are likely to be more effective in meeting needs and more efficient in using resources than one monopoly supplier. Thirdly, for there to be a variety of suppliers the public sector must operate in a way which allows the development of supply by non-government agencies. This carries a strong presumption against providing services free at the point of consumption. Where that is the case it will be very difficult for private and voluntary alternatives to develop.

The free public service will have to be very poor in quality or heavily rationed for alternatives to be able to compete. The immediate policy conclusion is that there should be a much more sustained effort to use public resources to develop a variety of suppliers. The key means is that of cash payments or vouchers together with incentives to suppliers to provide quality in services.

There is a vague and convenient view that choice can be extended while maintaining public monopoly, through improving information about services or through allowing clients to rank services such as schools in order of preference. There can be some useful gains from this but the limits have to be recognised. A monopoly supplier will tend to offer services of a similar kind. There are some differences between old people's homes, adult training centres and secondary schools but these differences should not be exaggerated. They are offering 'statutory' services staffed in rather the same way and with the same aims. Yet they are being offered in a society where the variety of household preferences of goods and services being produced in markets is increasing. Britain is now a much more diverse society in terms of social and ethnic groups and attitudes. The schools have had increasing and obvious difficulties with these changes. Households have access to knowledge, technology and training outside the official education system to a much greater extent than they did in the past. The needs of the disabled are sometimes put as an argument for public monopoly.

The greater pace of social and economic change of course means a great many difficulties for people with handicaps. The public aim is to help people live as normal a life as possible: but again public monopoly services are likely to be an ineffective way of helping them to do this. Unless they can use household resources and unless the full range of greater management ability in the community is mobilised on their behalf, the programmes are likely to create a new set of institutions on a smaller scale in the community.

If we define real choice in terms of the availability of services of different kinds, then there are some reasons for arguing that this must involve a variety of suppliers. The public monopoly can provide a minimum amount of consumption for all: but it cannot provide different services based on radically different ideas of how to provide the service. Given the shortage of tax finance it is also likely to be a heavily rationed service. Thus a decision for public monopoly is a decision in favour of providing a similar kind of service and one which must be subject to intense rationing by bureaucratic means.

The main argument for the monopoly public service has always been that it could meet need more fairly. This might be so where need can be measured by relatively objective physical criteria as with medical emergencies. But need in social settings is rarely so easy to measure. It has several characteristics which create difficulties for a monopoly. It is highly subjective. Different individuals can have very different feelings about the urgency of needs which seem the same in terms of measurable criteria. Secondly, need can often be measured in different ways which are fundamentally inconsistent. I came to see these points rather clearly as Chair of a Housing Management Committee with many people on a waiting list placed by quite a sophisticated points system. At one time in a mood of zeal just after taking over the assignment I had offers made to everybody on the list with more than 150 points. As it turned out about half of the people with these stupendously high points totally turned down the offers. Whatever the objective problems they preferred their current situation, their subjective reactions were quite different from those which the bureaucracy had expected. The other experience was that of trying to compare the housing needs of dissimilar groups with dissimilar problems. How to compare the housing needs of a young couple – who may have a very clear and intense need at present but very good prospects in the longer term – with the need of a middle-aged service worker on a low income? Under most bureaucratic systems the need of the young couple would have priority. But who can honestly say that any one, all-seeing bureaucracy could possibly produce one right ranking for these? There are different ways of measuring need which in practice are inconsistent.

A variety of suppliers with different aims and different interests are more likely to provide a certain amount for each and every one of the groups in need. Then the problem becomes the difficult, but more manageable one of deciding on priorities within different groups. Some housing associations will be interested in building housing for single people: others will build for young families. If the resources are there to be bid for, the supply of interest and commitment will be greater than is accessible to one monopoly supplier.

It is also sometimes argued that the public sector has some special ability to help the most disadvantaged. There is some practical evidence against this. For example some homes for the elderly – public as well as private – refuse places to people who are incontinent or confused. The record of voluntary groups in services for single homeless people in large cities has been much better than that of the public sector. But there are also some arguments of principle. The more 'difficult' the group the more important that services should be organised in a way that allows interest and initiative as free an entry as possible. A generic approach in which people are expected to help all 'problems' from drug addiction to mental confusion among elderly people is soon likely to exhaust anybody's capacity for sympathy. There may well be more people with special attitudes and empathy than can be attracted to work for one monopoly public service. The more difficult the group and the greater the difference of option about how to provide a service the more important that various different approaches be tried. The argument about services for mentally handicapped people has often seemed to imply that there was one right method of organising the service and that it was somehow wrong and anomalous that there should be radically different kinds of service financed through tax money. But such variety is essential to real progress and is again very difficult to achieve under a monopoly.

So far the argument has been about 'effectiveness' – the use of resources to meet client needs. But there is also a more common case against monopoly in terms of 'efficiency' – delivering an effective service at less cost. There has been a lot of argument about whether the public sector is inherently inefficient as compared to the private sector. There is a growing amount of evidence that the key factor is the degree of competition and that if public services are subject to more competition they can improve their efficiency (Milward, 1983). Where there is little competition and people are assured of the business with clients having nowhere else to go the incentives to efficiency are weak. The public sector also has a habit of developing special ways of doing things which raise cost. Thus social services have developed their own kinds of building both for day and for residential purposes. It is not easy to understand why they have not made much more use of ordinary housing. With the special language has gone a special architecture which tends to cut them off from day-to-day discourse and make for difficulties when the situation changes. Change can come about as has happened with the shift from children's homes to fostering, but it is very slow. The public sector may be able to achieve efficiency: but the balance of evidence suggests that variety in suppliers is more likely to provide favourable conditions for it.

There is much pious talk about the need for more choice in the public services: but this takes more than aspiration. It means that the economic conditions in which choice can develop have to be respected. It will be very difficult for non-governmental agencies to provide services where the public sector is giving services which are free or highly subsidised at the point of consumption. The point can be illustrated from the housing market. Council tenants have in the past paid rents which were too low to generate funds for maintenance: but the level of rents made it very difficult for voluntary groups and private firms to provide rented housing. It is only with the move to fair rents by housing associations that the supply of rented housing has increased. Any increase in the variety and quality of rented housing – in fact, any move towards a social market – will involve more 'economic' rent levels both in the public and in the private sector. The effects of free or subsidised services can also be seen in the market for training. There used to be a private market through which people could acquire office and other skills but because of competition from the colleges this has been almost eliminated. Choice can only develop where there is a variety of suppliers and a variety of suppliers can only develop where there is a pricing system which allows providers to operate long-term without subsidy.

All this suggests that the chosen fiscal methods of the future should be very different from those used in the past where the decision to finance a service publicly has usually led on to a decision to supply it through a public monopoly. There is still a strong case for public initiative in many areas to help people who do not have access to normal society and its markets. Social and economic disadvantage have deep and real effects on life chances: but the seriousness of the problem makes it more urgent to look for new ways in which public initiative can make a more effective contribution.

Tax money is now a scarcer resource, available only as a result of difficult reductions in other programmes or through increased taxation. That may be possible through inadvertence but will rarely be acceptable as a plan. The scarcity of tax money forces the question of output to the fore. It will be asked more often how much extra service can be derived from a given amount of tax money and the answer to this question will rarely favour old-style public enterprise. It will usually be possible to produce more output for a given amount of tax money by persuading others to come up with an additional finance. Thus interest is bound to grow in hybrid schemes using partly public and partly private finance.

There may be exceptions to the general rule against public monopoly. In the hospital services public monopoly may be better than the realistic alternative of an insurance-based system involving greater power to a professional monopoly. But in most other areas the balance of argument has shifted against the old-style public sector. Even the problems of regulation and of maintaining quality point against monopoly. The more difficult the problem the more important it is to have a variety of suppliers to ask to provide evidence on standards and achievements and to limit the scope for mishap.

The new fiscal method will involve essentially cash support and the provision of various types of voucher on the demand side, together with capital grants and loans to a variety of suppliers. This is a better economic constitution for a really effective programme against disadvantage.

References

Milward, R., 'The Comparative Performance of Private and Public Ownership', in Lord Rolls (ed.), *The Mixed Economy*, 1983.

Ritchie, J., Keegan, J. and Bosanquet, N., *Housing for Mentally Ill and Mentally Handicapped People*, HMSO, 1983.

4 Rights to Welfare
Kevin Carey

Just as feudal Christian social arrangements deteriorated via the Elizabethan Poor Law to the Dickensian workhouse, so the liberal welfare state has descended from initial high ideals to client-dependent empires of state bureaucracy. Should it ever take hold (and in spite of two terms of Thatcherism it has not done so yet, which only underlines the tenacity of the two traditions previously mentioned), the abrasive morality of self-determinism will fare no better.

In their way, feudalism, philanthropy and state provision have all had the same end in view – the maintenance of stability. At least in the Middle Ages there was some notion of a rights-based approach for although the giver and the receiver would not have considered themselves equal in any way, they did consider themselves to be in a contractual arrangement mirrored by the relationship between landowners and serfs; the contract might be harsh but both sides were equally bound to it by law and custom, Christian and secular.

Philanthropy, to put it at its most basic, existed primarily for two purposes, to give the philanthropist a sense of moral well-being and secondly, and much more important, to keep people off the streets. Both the Elizabethan Poor Law and the Dickensian workhouse had none of the first and a great deal of the second.

Looked at over a long perspective, the centralised provision of the modern state has some element in it of keeping people off the streets, of providing stability but its main purpose has been to guarantee mass-production. That universal compulsory education, adequate sanitation, better safety at work and a system of welfare payments have increased the general well-being of citizens is beyond doubt but the increase of benefit to individuals *per se* was never the primary moral objective. What was at stake was the viability of an industrial production system which required literate, healthy, reliable and docile labour. Only state-sponsored and state-financed provision could provide industry with these basic requirements.

It is ironic then, that the New Right is biting with such relish the hand that has fed its supporters. Abrasive individualism will no doubt confer short-term benefits on the better-off at the expense of the least advantaged but in the longer term, if such a trend persists, basic social stability is bound to break down to the disadvantage of everyone.

For all the apparent shifts over five centuries in attitudes to the relationship between the individual and the state, the underlying assumption has never changed. Though feudalism was contractual, the monarch, the peerage and the clergy were in authority over the lower orders and the laity respectively; there is no doubt, either, of the hierarchical arrangements with regard to Mr Bumble and Oliver Twist; and even though the New Left and the New Right are theoretically committed to the advancement of the rights of the community and the individual respectively *vis à vis* the state, there is no real chance of their achieving this in practice. The Right and the Left may disagree about the purposes for which the power of the centralised state may be used but that power, to parody a famous parliamentary resolution, has increased and is increasing under both the Labour and Conservative Parties; and, to complete the terms of the resolution, it ought to be diminished.

The vital, unifying factor in the operation of social arrangements in Britain has always been, and still is, the power of the owner of welfare finance, private or public, to determine the purposes for which it will be used. Admittedly, there have been some flat-rate cash payments like family allowance but the bulk of the 'social wage' has been sectored into a myriad of provisions in kind and specific means-tested cash benefits. The 'client' has been the central figure rather than the 'citizen'.

The notion of citizenship has been obscured by the fundamental assumption of political theorists and active politicians using the Left/Right model of politics that there is a fundamental antagonism between the enjoyment of greater individual liberty and the achievement of greater equality. In this situation the citizen is asked to choose between more of one or more of the other. If greater liberty is chosen, the position of the least advantaged deteriorates so that their liberty is ultimately only theoretical. If greater equality is chosen, the state/client relationship inevitably decreases the liberty not only, it should be noted, of the better-off who must finance the social engineering but also of the least advantaged who are forced into ever greater state dependence.

It is perhaps inevitable that such a situation has arisen in a nation whose central constitutional tenet is the sovereignty of Parliament. There is no basic notion of 'rights' in the British constitutional context; the citizen enjoys 'freedom', i.e. freedom to do what Parliament allows. Centralism, then, now perceived to have been at its zenith in the consensus of the 1950s, is not a new phenomenon but rather the culmination of a long process. The consensus was merely the confirmation of bipartisan acceptance of the Labour interpretation of the Liberal Party welfare state initiative at the beginning of this century.

Consensus, however, is not the same thing as consent. Further, as long as dominant political parties agree upon the role of the state (while they disagree on the uses to which it should be put), consent cannot be tested through the normal electoral process.

The arrangement of social affairs looks very different if a rights-based political structure is adopted. In this model, citizens have basic, non-negotiable rights. Acting alone, citizens cannot enjoy such rights to any great extent so they transmit authority upwards on a contractual basis to communities, regional authorities, sovereign nation-states and ultimately to supra-national bodies. In this model the key concept is the upward transmission of authority. The citizen only transmits upwards, or the smaller body only transmits upwards to a larger one, where the outcome will be an increase of enjoyment by the individual citizen of basic rights. Individual citizens have collectively decided to embark on a cooperative enterprise and therefore have an equal right to share in the fruits of that enterprise. The problematical factor is that to transpose an equal right into absolute equality may reduce the enjoyment of all citizens of their basic rights. Inequality may well be necessary for the social progress of the community as a whole but, at the same time, such inequality can only be justified on the basis that it is to the advantage of society as a whole and, most important, to the advantage of the least favoured (Rawls, 1972).

In the context of the social requirements required for the enjoyment by citizens of their basic rights, the upward transmission of authority model is in direct opposition to social engineering, religious or secular. This leads directly to a preference within such a system for the maximum amount of flexibility in achieving individual and community goals which in turn leads to a preference for money income over any kind of social wage or benefits in kind.

If a rights-based approach to social structures is accepted, neither the state nor any other authority is entitled to use its role as fund manager to determine how such funds are spent. Our current difficulty arises from the fact that central government has become a self-standing agency with its own concerns rather than being the repository of an upward transmission of authority from the citizen. It has recently become fashionable to assert that there is no such thing as 'government money', it is all 'taxpayers' money'; this is a good half-way to the truth. It is, in fact, 'citizens' money' rather than that of the taxpayer, for the taxpayer only arrives in the position to be able to pay tax because he or she operates inside a cooperative system. A job is created and filled by an individual as the result of countless inputs from individuals and groups over generations. The nostrum concerning the 'taxpayers' money' is also only half true because it is essentially the justification by the New Right for decreasing transfers from the better-off to the worse-off. In other words, while the apparent objective is to decrease the power of central government the actual outcome is a further erosion of the ability of the least advantaged to enjoy their basic rights.

Before developing the argument about the self-determination of the citizen and the use of cash rather than 'in kind' transfers, it should be noted that the position of children raises a special case. The area of children's 'rights' is extremely complex but if a position is adopted that people below a certain age are not full citizens but have certain rights then payments in kind may well be appropriate if that is the only way to overcome the chance of those rights being denied either by parents or by society as a whole. On this basis, for example, children may require statutory social services to compensate for parental neglect or maltreatment; education may need to be provided in kind or through a voucher system so that children from low-income families do not suffer disadvantage compared with children of better-off families. The situation for those in poor mental health is analogous. The essential point is that such measures apply to non-citizens; this term may appear to be rather harsh but it is in no way pejorative for all human beings have rights but some cannot participate in the two-way process of citizenship, the interplay between the individual and society.

If the moral imperialism of Christians, socialists and social engineers of all types are set aside, then the logical outcome is the use of cash-transfers as the method of distributing the fruits of social cooperation. The distribution criterion should be that it is as great as it possibly can be without jeopardising the prospects for improving the situation even further in the future; such a criterion at once justifies the accumulation of capital, and persistent inequality of income and wealth. The goose, so to speak, only justifies its existence as long as it continues to lay its golden eggs, with the majority of eggs being allocated to the least advantaged.

For the past quarter of a century there has been a tendency to divide economics into two branches, one dealing with advanced and the other with developing economies. While this may be justified in certain instances, it is remarkable how two basic propositions emerge across the whole spectrum of economies from the richest to the poorest. First, poverty results from a lack of income; secondly, the better the income distribution, the better the economic growth. The first proposition ought to be blindingly obvious but has been obscured in poor countries by discussions of food supply though it would not take a market economist long to track the food supply problem back to income; given income, the market would ensure the food supply. In richer countries moral imperialism – considerations of individual worth, idleness and so on – has been the obstacle to acceptance of the proposition. With regard to the second proposition, its rejection accounts in great part for the current economic and social difficulties being experienced by Britain.

It would be as well here to underline the difference between language and concept; the language which attacks social engineering – moral imperialism – may well sound like a proposition from the New Right but the concept it describes is radical. In as much as that concept, though radically distributive, is an attack on social engineering it is a quite distinctive position from that of socialism.

Although the primary distributive mechanism would be the establishment of a minimum but moving cash income for each person (children as well as adults), there would still have to be additional allowances based on need; seriously disabled people, for example, may require care and goods over and above those required by the 'standard' person. Cash-based redistribution, however, would do away with most of the current specific benefits which would, in turn, decrease the current discretion enjoyed by officials.

The environment required for such a system would be as radically different from the present as the system itself. A social system based on income distribution through the medium of cash would involve four important developments. The right to information, reform of the school curriculum, the 'separation of powers' between advisers on services and the providers of services and the fundamental redefinition of legal aid.

As noted above, there is a crucial difference between 'rights' and 'freedoms', and in this context it is unfortunate that so much has been written about the 'freedom of information'. It would be more constructive to deal with the 'right to information'. Government and local authority activity, including the compilation and analysis of data, is paid for by the citizen and deals with every aspect of the citizen. There will be cases, such as the confidentiality of personal records or of plans to preserve the security of the state, where the citizen will readily forgo the right to information but in all but these few cases the only bar to a right to information is the self-interest of a free-standing state which has rejected the notion of its contractual status. It is clear that in converting cash income into social services the citizen requires a wealth of information: current trends in disease, the safety of products, the description of problems anticipated and, following public discussion, the criteria on which a decision was taken to deal with them.

Obviously, an explosion in available data, together with a rights-based approach to society, would have a profound effect on the nature of the school curriculum. Learning facts in a rapidly changing society is already anachronistic but the curriculum would have to deal with techniques for finding and evaluating information to a much greater degree than it does at present. Perhaps even more difficult but necessary is the change of emphasis that would be required to deal with children as future citizens with equal rights.

A considerable proportion of the problems concerning the right to and evaluation of information would be eliminated through the separation of advisers or from providers of services. A cash-based system would make the ideological cleavage between state and private provision irrelevant; the two systems could compete (though it is likely that the private would gradually become dominant). Any configuration of service provision, but particularly one in which the state dominates, requires that the citizen should receive independent advice on the quality and cost of services. This would involve an extension of the 'named person' concept currently operating for some people to that of a 'personal advocate' paid for by the citizen (or the state where it has responsibility for children and others) out of the cash income of the citizen. Such an advocate would look after the interests of the citizen and would coordinate any multi-disciplinary approach to break the current circular referral syndrome.

One charge, however, which would not be met from individual income is that which results from the legal pursuit of rights. The ultimate forum in a rights-based as opposed to a freedom-based system is a court of law.

When a citizen brings an action in pursuit of rights or defends himself in an action against the claim of another then the activity should be termed as a constitutional duty rather than a right and, in as much as it is for the ultimate benefit of all citizens, it should be charged to the community as a whole.

Over and above any ideological objection to such a system the main consideration is bound to be the cost. There are two factors to be borne in mind here. The first is the amount of income currently available for distribution; 'cannot afford' generally means that political priorities run counter to whatever is being suggested. Further, such a system would involve a substantial saving of public expenditure. Secondly, the system proposed does not depend on the size of the cake, at least in the current British context. As national prosperity increases or declines, so would the basic income together with the amount available in the kitty to meet special needs.

It might be argued that the nature of the outcome of the system for individuals would be uncertain. This is, of course, true but certainty of outcome can only be achieved through the imposition of one morality or one view upon an individual or group. Conversely, social services would be oriented towards fulfilling the potential of the citizen rather than making up for 'deficits' determined by what society thinks a citizen should be or do.

No matter how the subject is approached, it is impossible to escape from the central tension between the citizen and the state, between choice and paternalism, between rights and freedoms, between law interpreted in open court and regulations interpreted behind closed doors. The second component of each of these antitheses might have been required by a state whose primary source of wealth was standardised mass-production but both justice and future prosperity in the high technology environment demand the primacy of the first components. The production of wealth is, after all, the outcome of cooperative social arrangements rather than the arbiter of them.

Part II
Welfare

Introduction

Pursuing and achieving a satisfactory organisational model which will both maximise the role of welfare consumers, and at the same time be allowed to work, is probably one of the most difficult but important developments to be made within current public services. It is not the only desirable objective to be pursued: an adequate funding base is equally vital and, we would argue, closely bound up with the future of consumerist values in all of the major services which are examined in the section which follows. Significant changes in the way local authority finance, for example, has been organised will flow from changes in the rates system – themselves in part engendered by and engendering a consumerist approach to local government provided services.

But models can be argued about, debated and toyed with endlessly. What by themselves they cannot do is provide the impetus towards the changes so many seek. Consumerists come in all shapes and sizes and, as our section shows, have no single particular argument or organisational model in common. What they have instead is the common belief that the consumers of a service should, collectively and singly, have a greater say in the way in which that service is run, and greater control over the standards and objectives it pursues.

To that end each of our contributors have devoted their chapters. Jef Smith's proposals (chapter 8) – and it is odd that in social services such eminently reasonable suggestions should sound desperately radical to some ears – should be tested say in two or three authorities on an experimental basis. For surely it is the reluctance of the present government to experiment in anything like imaginative ways which has given the ideological lie to the crude, political populism that can so often masquerade as consumerism proper.

Finally none of our authors considered (it wasn't in their brief) the extent to which enhancing the power of consumers inevitably means a loss of power for those who currently control those services. Teachers, medical staff, social workers and housing officials daily take decisions on our behalf and the sole rationale for those decisions can only be that they are made in our – the consumers – best interests. What seems likely, in the struggle which is bound to loom in the coming decade and for which we, in a sense, have to thank the New Right for however clumsily unleashing, is that the battlefield will increasingly be concerned with who shall define those interests, and how.

On the one hand, there might persist an increasingly defensive and frustrated band of public sector professionals, anxiously seeking to defend its powers and privileges while seeing its status continuously downgraded. On the other, the increasingly offensive and frustrated purchasers of goods which will be available both from public as well as private suppliers. In those circumstances, and with the local authority base of those professionals being systematically eroded, we argue now as we have argued before: it is time for those professionals to seize the opportunities consumerism offers – to go out and welcome their customers in a way in which all their previous securities and privileges have made them forget. It is only in the development of a new consensus between consumer and supplier that the future and quality of our welfare services will in any way be assured.

5 Education
Anne Sofer

Defining the Terms

Who are the consumers of education? This is not as simple as it sounds. For a start there has been a growing tendency in recent years to see education as an 'investment' rather than a service. This has come from all political sides, and for different reasons. From the Right, spending on education is seen as 'money down the drain' unless there are hard results for the national economy in terms of 'marketable skills'. The 'consumers' on this model would be the investors, i.e. the taxpayer, represented by central government, and advised by the employers. From the other side of the political spectrum, the vocabulary of investment is called in chiefly to justify increases in spending – this line of argument also emphasises jobs, the needs of the economy, and deploys the statistics of skill shortages and unfavourable international comparison.

This leaves many, particularly those professionally engaged in education, uneasy. To them, education is an individual right, justified in terms only of itself. Knowledge and enlightenment increase the power and autonomy of the individual, and are as integral to human development as health. Such people would see the 'consumer' (though they would not like the word) as the child, and later the adult. While the child is dependent it is the professional teacher who is the best interpreter of his/her needs, though even at this stage he/she should have maximum choice. The parent may be a partner in this exercise, but not a consumer.

A third group, while not denying that education is both an investment and a right, prefers always to see education as a 'service', but the sort of service that has masters rather than consumers. That is not as subservient as it sounds. On the contrary, like the civil 'service', it puts the servants at one remove from the consumers. People enter the education service as they might enter the Church: they devote themselves to ministering to the needs of the people but the terms of the 'service' itself defines those needs. This group talks the language of response, but it is the response to need, not demand; and the decisions about response to need are not taken at the point at which they express themselves but elsewhere in political and bureaucratic processes. This group also is antipathetic to the language of the market being imported into education. Education is too much a matter of principles, they say, to be defined in terms of commercial practices.

A jumble of all three attitudes probably co-exists in the public mind and in the heightened and politically charged atmosphere that surrounds education at present, the messages reaching teachers about what they are supposed to be doing must sound at times like a badly-tuned radio at top volume. In fact, this no doubt contributes to their current demoralisation. As far as the pupils are concerned, at any rate those between 5 and 16, any perception of themselves as consumers is complicated by the element of compulsion. Can a conscript ever be described as a consumer? For their parents, compulsion has, if anything, sharpened the consumerist approach: if their children have to attend, at least let them have more say about it all.

What do we mean by 'consumerism'? My own definition would include three essential elements: diversity and choice, quality control and what I can only call 'motivated purchasing'. The first of these elements will be well understood; by 'quality control' I mean all the means by which the consumer checks on the quality and value for money of what he is buying and has the means of redress for shoddy goods. The last element, 'motivated purchasing', is intended to describe the essential state of mind a consumer must be in: he must want what he is buying (whether or not that want has been artificially induced), and he must make sure he knows how to use it before he completes the purchase.

Reflection on these three elements separately brings the realisation that for each element, as for each stage of education, there is a mix of consumers involved. For the first two elements, as far as schools are concerned, it is the parent who is the consumer: for the last it is the child, although the child may very well be heavily affected by the parents' attitude. For people over the school-leaving age, the student is the chief consumer, though in some respects his choice, his access to information and his attitude will be heavily conditioned by other influences, notably employers.

How responsive is the education system to these consumers? Could it be more so? Before looking at the possible answers to this question under the headings of fiscal consumerism, organisational consumerism, and individual consumerism, let us look for a moment at the reality.

The Reality

One way of looking at reality is to imagine a child, setting out for the first time to school: it should be a touching, hopeful sight, with the feel of misty dawn and a bright day ahead.

An illusion? Well, it depends on the child. Let us pick one at random. This one is called Sharon, and she is just five, picking her way through the puddles this rainy September morning, clutching apprehensively her mother's hand. She is the youngest of four children, and her father left her mother a year ago. Her mother will try to stay for a few minutes to 'settle' her in the reception class, but then she will have to hurry off to work: she has taken an hour off this morning especially; tomorrow Sharon will be brought in by her nine-year-old brother. Sharon's mother will take a minute to collect a form to fill in for free school meals – even working full-time her income is low enough to give her full entitlement – and she will sit down trying to understand it while Sharon is being induced to join in with the other children.

There is one other new child this morning, Henry. Henry comes in with his nanny and doesn't cling to her even for a moment. He is raring to go: he already knows some of the children from the nursery class. Sharon's mother did not send her to the nursery class for its hours did not fit in with her working day. Sharon was looked after by a child-minder up the road.

They both proceed, six years later, into the local comprehensive. (Henry's parents, affluent professionals who could afford the private sector, have a strong political commitment to state education.) Sharon continues to qualify for free school meals. Henry participates in the school orchestra and the school play and represents his class on the school council. Sharon gets disaffected and falls into bad company. She gets caught glue-sniffing. The police, the educational welfare service, the educational psychologist all have files on her. Once every couple of months they take out their files and consider her case. Someone tentatively suggests a special school. Sharon and her mother, both appalled, have a rare meeting of minds in fiercely resisting such a proposal. A deal is struck: Sharon attends school just enough to prevent the professionals feeling they have to do something. She even pretends she is going to take a few CSEs. But she leaves school thankfully at Easter, draws the dole as quickly as she can, and thus adds perceptibly to the family standard of living.

Six months later, bored, she tentatively investigates doing a typing course at the local further education college. But when she hears she would have to give up her dole money she gives up the idea. She avoids the careers office, not wanting to be placed on a YTS scheme, having heard nothing good about them. Some of the time she is not unhappy – at least nobody is hassling her any more. But when things get bad between her and her mother, she dreams of getting pregnant so that she and her boyfriend can get a council flat and set up home on their own ...

Henry meanwhile joins the local authority's junior orchestra and travels to Spain and Portugal on a concert tour. He passes seven 'O' levels with high grades and stays on into the sixth. He has developed something of a hobby in computers, but since he took no physical sciences at 'O' level (when he chose his options at 13, he'd just had a row with the physics teacher) he settles for arts 'A' levels. On a special scheme to encourage youngsters from inner city comprehensives to go to Oxford, he gets a place at Balliol to read PPE. His three years at Balliol are extended to five through his election to two successive sabbatical offices as an officer of the student union. He gets a job on a Fleet Street paper but he has his eye on Parliament.

Now let us do some arithmetic. In round figures, and in the real terms of

1985/86, Sharon's education will cost the state in all £13,500: six years of primary education at £1000 a year, and five years of secondary education at £1500 a year. (This is a generous, though not the most generous, progressive authority.) Henry's education will cost the state £40,900 – almost precisely three times as much. To Sharon's basic statutory minimum must be added two years of nursery education at £1200, and five years of higher education at £5000. If the campaign that Henry is currently waging for the abolition of the 'parental contribution' to student grants had been successful earlier he would be getting an extra £10,000 on top of that. Furthermore, Henry has emerged from the education system with an earning power, within a few years, of £12,000. Sharon's earning power is something between nil and £3000.

Not surprisingly, Sharon and Henry feel differently about the education system. Sharon, after the first few years in the primary school, began to feel first a passenger, then an intruder, and finally a reject from institutions to which she hardly seemed to belong. Henry absorbed from his parents the notion that he was conferring by his very presence a benefit on the publicly-funded schools and his academic success was a triumphant vindication of his parents' public-spiritedness. Henry's mother spent a lot of time over the years agitating for a PTA and serving as a parent governor.

These portraits, although they describe opposite ends of the spectrum, are not caricatures. Most teachers would recognise both of them. And although this essay is not about inequality, it is impossible to examine any proposition about either the state of the present education system or any possible improvements to it without facing up to the facts of inequality. The existing model of 'education as a service responsive to need' seems to have a depressing tendency to reinforce that inequality. Could a consumerist approach do any better?

Fiscal Consumerism

Some people, contemplating Sharon's history, might be tempted to argue that she would have been better off with the money, rather than the education. Short of abolishing compulsory education, this is not an available alternative; but it should be noted that at at least two points in Sharon's life, more money would have made a difference to her educational chances. If her mother had not had to work full-time, she would have had the benefit of nursery education; and if she had had some form of financial maintenance, she might have enrolled on that typing course. A higher level of child benefit and an amendment to the supplementary benefit regulations could have significantly improved her life chances. An egalitarian wanting to improve Sharon's opportunities as a consumer of education, would do so via the DHSS, not via the education service. A fierce and radical egalitarian, however, looking at the sums of money absorbed in educating Sharon and Henry respectively, would soon come up against some very sacred cows.

Take the sum for nursery education, for instance. Only around 40 per cent of three to five year olds nationally have the benefit of nursery education at present and the government does not intend to allow that proportion to increase. Pre-school playgroups, some subsidised, cater for a substantial further proportion. But there is no way of ensuring that those children who need it most, and whose parents cannot afford to buy it, are getting it. The idea of 'pre-school vouchers', cashable at any approved establishment at hours and times convenient to the parent, would no doubt appall. As far as I know, it has never been floated. Yet it is one way a more flexible and comprehensive provision could be encouraged to develop. It would even be possible to redistribute existing resources in order to achieve this. Sharon's mother would be given a voucher big enough to pay for full-time nursery class; Henry's parents would have to contribute some of the cost of the part-time session themselves.

Any proposal to redistribute post-school education spending similarly would no doubt also be met with cries of horror. Yet higher education already operates according to a sort of voucher system – for some. The Robbins principle means, in fact, that any student with at least two 'A' levels has an entitlement to three years' full-time study cashable at a wide choice of institutions. There is no reason in theory why such an entitlement should not be extended to the entire population, with a wider range of courses and institutions. The cost would be prohibitive, and could only be met by redistribution – say one year for all, and a system of loans to cover any study after that. The political outcry that would greet any such proposal makes it impossible to discuss as a practical proposition.

The form of fiscal consumerism that has had the most exposure and the best hope of implementation, has been the 'education voucher' for school education. Some Conservative radicals saw it as a way of giving all parents freedom of choice, and of putting unpopular schools on warning that unless they improved their performance they would close. The idea failed partly because of the united opposition of the education establishment, but also partly because of the inherent impracticability of the proposals. Unlike a 'product' which sells well, most schools cannot quickly 'respond to demand' by increasing output overnight: there is not space. So any school system has to have an allocation system which has a worked-out set of priorities in the case of over-subscribed schools.

A more basic flaw in the 'voucher' idea can be illustrated by reference to our two examples. The idea, after all, is in theory that all parents would be able to 'buy' private education if they wanted to. But a moment's consideration will make clear that, whereas Henry's parents could probably have bought him a place at one of the top independent schools, Sharon's mother would have had no such access. If schools in a voucher system (as opposed to parents) are doing the choosing, then inequalities merely increase. Although parents who managed to get their children accepted at 'good' schools would presumably be more satisfied, those who found their children rejected, perhaps again and again, would become sadly demoralised and embittered.

Nobody in this country has suggested a totally fair voucher system. An

American guru of the voucher movement, Professor Sugarman, has put forward an ideal of pure voucherism which would involve all schools participating in surrendering control of admissions, and the problem of over-subscription being determined by lot. This is logical and honest, but – unfortunately perhaps – political cloud cuckoo-land.

The government has retracted from vouchers and opted for a very much smaller experiment in 'fiscal consumerism' – the assisted places scheme. This merely extends the privilege of opting out to a very small number, without bringing any more choice into the system as a whole.

But I would not entirely write off 'fiscal consumerism' as a means to improving both quality and equality in education. Outside the statutory years, there is a case for some pilot experiments targeted particularly at those groups in the population, like Sharon, who are hardly at all motivated at present to purchase any education, and who know very little about the choices open to them. If, for instance, an entitlement to one year's full-time education or training (or its part-time equivalent) were made available to all adults who had left school at the minimum leaving age and had had no further education since, what might be the result? One would hope that not only would some individuals, who might have matured and developed in the interim, seize the opportunity with both hands, but also, and more importantly, some institutions would start thinking hard and creatively about how to attract to themselves that education 'spending money' that would suddenly be available in a part of the community that they have not customarily catered for.

There is one other development which, with some stretching of the meaning, I would like to discuss under the heading of 'fiscal consumerism'. This is the devolution of spending decisions from bureaucracies to institutions.

If an institution – in this case a school – can be seen as the sum of all its users, then a move in this direction can be seen as a move in the direction of 'consumerism'. In the case of private schools, and to a lesser extent voluntary aided schools, institutional autonomy already exists. The school 'buys in' from the money it has available, some of the services it needs. Some education authorities have also given a degree of virement within total sums to their individual schools. Within this group of semi-autonomous education institutions one would also find some of the bodies that subsist on a combination of grants, fund-raising and voluntary work, like playgroups and youth clubs.

What all these bodies have in common is some form of local decision-making on the disposal of funds, which must involve the consumers, the representatives of the consumers, rather than the elected bureaucracy. The governing bodies and management committees will be closer to the competing demands in the specific circumstances of the school than are the politicians, who will have their own ideas about priorities.

Nobody is suggesting that the politicians, whether central or local, should abandon their role of determining the relative allocation of public funds between institutions: but a number of voices are raised to support the idea of a far greater local control over the disposal of the allocated amount within each institution. In Cambridgeshire, a pilot scheme of 'local financial management' (Burgess, 1983) has been tried in a number of schools and is likely to be extended shortly to the whole authority.

Inside Local Government (Henney, 1984) makes a number of radical suggestions for making local services more consumer-oriented by proposing an extreme form of this model. The school would determine what ancillary services it wanted to use – whether, for instance, it wanted to spend £5000 a year on education welfare services and educational psychologist back-up, or whether it would prefer to use that money in some other way. This would, of course, revolutionise these services, turning them from a professional department answerable to bureaucracies and ultimately politicians, into consultancy services, answerable to heads and ultimately governors and working on a piece-rate, freelance basis.

To try to imagine what difference this might make, let us look at Sharon again. When she got into trouble, Sharon's school passed the problem on to the specialist agencies: we do not know how satisfied the school was, but at least the problem was contained. More importantly, we do not know whether the school, given the choice, would have spent the money resolving the problem differently. Nor do we know whether, if it had total discretion over its funding, it would have chosen to spend any of its money at all solving Sharon's problems. It was Henry's mother, after all, not Sharon's, who had a seat on the governing body. On the other hand, some would argue that it would be wrong to assume that the public-spirited middle-class parent activist would manipulate the system even more to the benefit of her own kind than the progressive bureaucracies are already doing. Is it not possible (they might say) that the decisions made at local level would be at least as fair, and might – because they would be more closely monitored – be more effective? These are questions it is impossible to answer, and there will be fierce partisans on either side of the argument. But the Cambridgeshire experiment, and any further extension of it, should be watched closely.

Organisational Consumerism

Other branches of the public services often look to education as having the ready-made model of organisational consumerism. The individual school governing body seems the perfect vehicle for consumer representation. It is interesting that Sir Keith Joseph, when he was finally driven to abandon the idea of education vouchers, started looking to the governing body as the means through which consumer influence would be felt. His first proposal was for a majority of parents on governing bodies; he has now pulled back from this position, under pressure of opinion, and is proposing to legislate for governing bodies on which parents have a sizeable, but not an overriding, number of places. The current proposals are not far from what the Taylor Committee of Inquiry recommended in 1977, and what most relevant pressure groups, like the Campaign for the Advancement of State Education (CASE), and the National Association of Governors and Managers (NAGM) had been campaigning for since the early 1970s.

This history is significant in that it indicates the progress of a gathering consensus on this issue of 'organisational consumerism'. There has never been, in England, a head of steam behind a full-blown consumerist approach to the governance of schools. Unlike the United States, where parent organisations nationally are far more influential; or, say, Denmark, where relatively small groups of parents can actually attract almost total subsidy for schools run by themselves, the parent movement in this country has never claimed more than partnership status – the partnership being with the teachers, and sometimes, more reluctantly, with the politicians.

Whether this is because of a habit of deference towards teachers in this country, or because the vocabulary of partnership caught hold in the progressive primary schools of the 1950s and 1960s and spread from there, or because the early parent organisations were blessed with diplomatic skills, I find it hard to judge. The fact remains that even on those governing bodies where parents are most strongly represented, the prevailing climate of opinion gives as much weight to 'producer' (i.e. teacher) interests as to 'consumer' (i.e. parent) interests. Indeed, in the atmosphere of the 1970s and early 1980s of cuts and closures, a solidarity of interest in defence of the individual school was the most common relationship between the two groups. The teachers' industrial action of 1985–6, the first phenomenon with the potential to drive a wedge between the two groups, did not in fact do so. Parent governors, although no doubt aware of the problems their fellow parents were facing, behaved with great circumspection in their relationship with the teachers and the teachers' unions. The National Confederation of Parent-Teacher Associations, when it did at one stage call on the teachers to call off the strike, was immediately denounced by the other parents' organisations and some of its own members.

An awareness of the partnership relationship characterises most of the public pronouncements of the national parents' organisations – indeed, the chief one, the National Confederation of Parent Teacher Associations is by its very constitution an embodiment of that relationship. Where parents have been given some sort of formal position within the consultative arrangements of local education authorities, they are also in this situation highly conscious of teacher interests. For instance, in the Inner London Education Authority, where there is a structure of local and central parents' consultative committees, consisting of elected parent governors, the Central Parents' Consultative Committee took an initiative over the teachers' pay disputes, and approached the Secretary of State to urge him to promote a settlement in the spring of 1985. They took care, however, to coordinate their action with the teachers' associations in Inner London, so that the initiative could be seen as a joint approach. A similar plan of campaign was adopted in the London Borough of Richmond by parent activists.

A recent report of a Brunel University research team into school governing bodies draws somewhat depressing conclusions about the effectiveness of parent governors – how far they are able to represent the mass of parents or to stand up to the more weighty vested interests of teachers and political groupings. Since parent governors are a relatively recent innovation it would be wrong to be depressed too soon. It 's probably only realistic to assume that they will have to operate within the 'consensualist' or 'mini-corporatist' climate that characterises the English education system; but possible to work for a strengthening of their position within that framework.

There are almost no examples of 'parent power' trying to exercise its muscles on its own. Much was made at the 1985 Conservative Party Conference of 'parental anger' on the issue of political indoctrination. But as Sir Keith Joseph admitted in his speech on that occasion, he can take no action without evidence and though there is certainly some unease, it is vague and unsubstantiated. The 'backlash against left-wing teachers' which the Conservatives are clearly pinning great hopes on, has failed to produce any organised lobby. Indeed, most of those who make the loudest noise are not parents of children in the maintained sector of education.

There is one source of parent attack on the system which is more real, but politically of a very different complexion. I refer to the various black community groups who have become increasingly uninhibited in expressing their belief that English teachers have consistently sold their children short. These groups have not, so far, been absorbed into the consensual partnership, and they attack with equal vigour the Conservative government and the various Labour councils who often seem publicly to be going out of their way to placate them. A particularly virulent publication, *Black Parent*, is circulating in London at present. Perhaps the most visible achievement of this type of protest to date is the furore surrounding the suspension and precarious reinstatement of the Bradford headmaster, Ray Honeyford. What this saga illustrates is that parents can be roused to make their presence as consumers felt, and that when that happens they will attempt to use parent governorships as one of the levers of power.

In fact, most head teachers would say even now that parents have a strong influence over how they run their schools – not just through the parent governors or parent–teacher associations, but through the informal feedback of individual parental complaints, anxieties or (more rarely) congratulations. Most heads would also admit that this influence has strengthened over recent years, not least because, with school rolls falling in most parts of the country, market forces have been operating. Declining popularity carries with it the risk of closure. So far, parents exercise greater control over the system through the sum of their individual choices than through any organised representational mechanism.

'Organisational consumerism' exists outside the statutory years of schooling. One of the great successes of the voluntary movement in the post-war years has been the Pre-School Playgroup Association – an organisation run by consumers. Established to fill a gap, rather than to compete with a professionally run service, it had the time and space to develop the particular strengths of a consumer-run service, and played a considerable role in establishing the concept of 'parents as educators' which is now beginning to permeate educational thinking, if not practice.

At the other end of the age span, the consumer role of students has not yet been satisfactorily developed. The 'student revolutions' of 1968 produced a rash of reforms to governing bodies and academic boards but with little visible impact, and student union activities tend to concentrate either on purely social organisation or, on the other hand, on national political issues. As a vehicle for students' views on educational quality and relevance they are relatively ineffective.

In one sense, of course, it is not the students but their future employers who are the 'consumers' of higher education. Their role in determining the content of degree courses is highly controversial. Broadly speaking the Left view has been that the business world must not be allowed to interfere with academic freedom in any way, and that the presence of industrialists on the governing councils of universities is a sinister threat. The Right view, particularly as represented by the present Conservative government, has been quite the reverse: large sections of the recent Green Paper on Higher Education are devoted to discussing how business and industry can be more influential within higher education.

It is only recently that public opinion in this country has become aware that in other countries which are prospering to a greater extent than we are, industry's role in the national education and training system is taken for granted, and employers both invest in, and influence the curriculum content of, considerable proportions of what is on offer to young people. *Competence and Competition* (NEDO/MSC, 1984), the report prepared by the Institute of Manpower Studies for the Manpower Services Commission and the National Economic Development Council, describes in some detail the constitutional and economic arrangements in the United States, West Germany and Japan. It is a characteristic of this country that neither side – the education nor the business worlds – really wants this close relationship. The education world is afraid of a 'tainting' influence: the business world does not want to pay.

To conclude this section on 'organisational consumerism', let us look back at the two examples of reality, Sharon and Henry, and see how they might be affected by any of the developments described here. To take Sharon first: she would probably have benefited greatly from a pre-school playgroup that involved her mother if such an organisation had existed in her area, and if its hours had fitted in better with her mother's working life than the local nursery did. That is at present a possibility but not a strong one. The pre-school playgroup movement tends to be stronger in suburban and rural areas, often because it is those areas that are the most poorly provided for by the state (though they have had notable successes in some inner city multi-racial areas, e.g. Southall in West London).

It is hard to argue from the evidence so far that Sharon might have been helped by a stronger representation of parents on the school governing body, at least in the short term. Her mother probably did not go to the meeting to elect parent governors (did Sharon even give the notice to her?), and probably does not know who the parent governor is. However, it is at least possible that the parents would have picked up the worries about glue-sniffing earlier than the teachers; or could have pressured the school into having a better general system of contact with parents. Long term, the potential is there.

What certainly would have helped Sharon would have been some employer input into the post-16 provision of her education. In West Germany, for instance, it would not have been so easy for her to drift. An apprenticeship system, organised and financed jointly by employers and the state, would have been the natural next stage of her career.

As for Henry, he is one of the winners under the present system. But even his story is an example of wasted opportunities. Participation in a consumer interest group (the student union) became for him, as for so many, a step onto a political career ladder. And meanwhile, near the beginning of his educational progress, a possible alternative way forward had been blocked, paradoxically, by too much choice. But this takes us on to the next section.

Individual Consumerism

Henry had been allowed to give up the study of the physical sciences at the age of 14, thus cutting off the possibility of pursuing a career in science, medicine, engineering and a number of other fields. His hobby in computers indicates he may have had an aptitude, and his parents may have tried to argue him out of the decision. None the less, he took it, at this very tender age, as does about half the age group every year (though most of them are girls).

In fact, the idea of 'consumer choice' has been very fashionable within the curriculum for the last 30 years. Both at the primary school level, where the idea of children choosing from a range of different learning experiences is integral to much modern teaching methods, and at secondary level, where one of the early benefits that used to be cited in favour of the large comprehensive school was the great range of options spread out like a tempting cornucopia before the young citizens of tomorrow. Enthusiasm has now cooled, as it became clear that choice needs some constraint if potential is to be fulfilled and career paths left open. The goal of unfettered individual choice and the goal of a good basic education for all have been discovered not to coincide.

A similar perplexity attends the idea of parental choice of school. Under the law, parents can express a preference for a school, and they can appeal to a specially constituted appeal body if they fail to gain a place. This much was laid down in the Conservatives' Education Act 1980, which clarified the vaguer position under the 1944 Act. But the 1980 Act also gave local authorities power to fix a maximum size for each school, and so for a school which is over-subscribed, both the choice and the appeal becomes for some parents meaningless.

After the appeal decision, parents can complain to the Secretary of State, or go to the Ombudsman. The Secretary of State is very unlikely to intervene (unless there are some particularly strong political pressures) and the Ombudsman can only uphold a complaint if the local authority has actually disregarded its own regulations and procedures.

It is, in fact, administratively impossible to run a choice system for parents which gives everyone what they want: this is not only because of the problem of some schools not having the physical capacity for all the children whose parents want them to go there. There are also cases where parental wishes conflict with each other. It is a well-known phenomenon for instance that parents will choose single-sex schools for their daughters and co-educational schools for their sons.

A pressing problem facing many local education authorities is whether or not to respond to the demand coming from some sections of society for separate new religious schools. The Catholics and the Church of England fought a long and bitter battle to retain their right to run their own schools with public money which they won in the famous settlement of 1944. Under these arrangements for 'voluntary schools', the Jews also established their own denominational schools. Some Moslem groups are now pressing for the same right and the claim is hard to resist; although fears of racial separatism are strong.

On this issue, a comparison with practice in other countries reveals our own arrangements in a favourable light. In both the United States and France, where separate religious schools are not part of the maintained system, they have become to some extent a privileged private sector, and a source of social as well as sectarian division. At least the English system has avoided this – though some would claim that it had not.

A jealously guarded privilege of most voluntary aided schools is that they have the right to expel a pupil: a county school can be overriden in this respect by the local education authority. In 1985 the schools of Manchester were in uproar over the case of five boys expelled from Poundswick High School for executing obscene graffiti on the school's elevation, whom the education committee has ordered to be reinstated. If Poundswick were a voluntary aided school, there would be no question of this happening. Parents are often attracted to voluntary aided schools not because of the religious ethos but because they know the school does not have to take all comers. 'Consumerism' can sometimes mean the urge to get away from the other consumers.

So choice and diversity are two-edged instruments, and it is likely that the system will continue much as it is, with local authorities trying to walk the tightrope between administrative good sense and parents' wishes. That being so, what of the other two features of consumerism – quality control and 'motivated purchasing'?

The flow of information about the quality and availability of education in this country is not impressive. The 1980 Act made it compulsory for schools to publish their examination results and certain other facts about the school but there is no standardisation about the way this is done and no way of comparing 'like with like' in terms of a school's performance. The education establishment has a rooted dislike of the publication of 'league tables' for fear that they will only further reinforce social difference between schools. Government and other research has established time and again that social background is the main determinant of academic success. In the ILEA however, a sophisticated measure of examination success has been developed which takes account of social background and ability distribution on entry to secondary school. This does indeed produce a league table, which contains some surprises. It is so direct and easy to understand that the idea of its publication causes considerable nervousness. So far it has not even been discussed.

What the system lacks is an adequate system of redress for complaints. In two cases I have taken up recently for constituents, a complaint from a parent to the education officer (in the one case in connection with poor quality of teaching, in the other with breach of confidence by a teacher) was met with a threat of legal action from the teacher complained of. Understandably, both parents backed off – and these were among the minority that brought themselves to the point of complaining. Many, however unjustifiably, fear victimisation of their children if they register a complaint. It may be that an entirely new procedure is needed, something like a 'parents' ombudsman' who would not be part of the hierarchy of the education service.

But devising a procedure that gives parents a full say in decisions relating to their children's education is not easy. An official attempt to do so is the 1981 Education Act concerning children with special needs. This, while giving parents of handicapped children a much more central role, has produced a procedure which is both cumbersome and long-winded.

Other parts of the education system too are slow to promote information about themselves. It has been left to a private researcher to compile year after year the information about university entrance which sixth form students and their teachers most want to know – what the chances of admission in the various subjects actually are. When Brian Heap (1985) first started doing this work he had to go about collecting his data in the most circuitous way: the educational institutions themselves were very wary of giving it to him.

An Audit Commission (1985) report on Value for Money in Further Education has recently castigated the further education colleges for their lack of a 'marketing approach'. The section is worth quoting in full.

'An effective marketing effort by a college is likely to require the following:
(a) Senior time and effort. Many FE establishments are sizeable operations in their own right with a cost base appropriate to companies with sales of £5m a year or more. Such companies would have one or two senior executives assigned full-time to understanding the market they are seeking to serve and devising ways in which their products can be made attractive and relevant to changing market needs. Colleges face similar challenges and require similar expertise.
(b) Market intelligence. Any college needs a clear understanding of what its users

think they want and how they view the present range of courses being offered. At minimum, it will be essential to obtain their views on the present courses and likely future changes in demand through regular (at least annual) interviews with local Job Centres, major local employers (especially those participating in the Youth Training Scheme). Manpower Services Commission. Local secondary schools and trades unions.

(c) Feedback. It is difficult to see how colleges can understand how well individual courses are meeting the needs of the market unless they make systematic attempts to obtain specific feedback from the market place. This could take the form of:

— a student report at the end of each session;
— 'exit' interviews with students dropping out; why do individuals not continue on courses for which they have enrolled?
— follow-up with students who have completed courses, say six months later: with hindsight (which is always improved) how could the course have met their needs better?

What this passage brings home is an essentially 'free enterprise' message. The 'demand economy' consumerist approach has to find out what people want and have a sophisticated system of feedback, so that it can change its product. The 'command economy' approach gives people what it thinks they need, and has only limited systems for assessing customer satisfaction.

Whether this is fair judgement or not, it is certainly true that remarkably little market research is done on the recipients of education and training. Anecdotal evidence and ordinary observation tell us that particularly from 14 to 16 there is a considerable amount of dissatisfaction, but actual evidence on what is wanted, or what might work better, is thin on the ground. Teachers follow their own hunches - sometimes with considerable flair - but with insufficient evidence.

And so how, finally, are we to enhance this third feature of consumerism - 'motivated purchasing'? How are we to ensure that people positively want education and know how to use it? It is clear that we are particularly weak as a nation in this respect. Two key recent publications stress, in their different ways, this very point. The Hargreaves Report on secondary schools in Inner London defines four aspects of achievement: the first three are academic achievement, problems-solving and personal and social competence. But the fourth 'achievement aspect IV' underpins all the others.

This aspect of achievement involves motivation and commitment; the willingness to accept failure without destructive consequences; the readiness to persevere; the self-confidence to learn in spite of the difficulty of the task. Such motivation is often regarded as a prerequisite to achievement, rather than as an achievement in itself. We do not deny that motivation is a prerequisite to the other three aspects of achievement, but we also believe that it can be regarded as an achievement in its own right. For some pupils come to their schools without such motivation, yet the school succeeds in generating it in them and in such circumstances, both the school and the pupils have made an important achievement. By contrast, some schools actively reduce the motivation and commitment of pupils, thereby causing further under-achievement in aspects I-III. In one sense, aspect IV is the most important of all, since without it achievement in the other three aspects is likely to be very limited, both at school and in the future. Working-class pupils are particularly vulnerable here, since some of them, because of disadvantaged circumstances come to school with already low levels of aspect IV achievement; they rely upon teachers, in a way that most middle-class pupils do not for immediate and basic help with aspect IV. If the school does not attend to aspect IV as a central feature of its work, then achievement in the other three aspects becomes improbable. When the school believes it is not within its powers to influence aspect IV, the teachers begin to explain the lack of achievement in terms of the pupils' background and these lower teacher expectations become self-fulfilling. And when pupils experience their schooling as a threat to their aspect IV achievement, it becomes rational for them to play truant or to protect themselves by classroom misbehaviour.

Competence and Competition (NEDO/MSC 1984) reports from its comparison of our system with the United States, West Germany and Japan the 'unexpected research finding' that in all three countries the 'pro active role' expected of the individual was high.

> Individuals are encouraged to continue work-related education and training. Leading employers in the three countries achieve this in different ways but their aims are the same: commitment, team work, continuous learning and adaptability as part of the management of work, supported by relevant training activities.

To change our own demotivated climate will need a number of different measures and a concerted effort, starting not least with a government that will give a strong message to the country that it believes in education and is prepared to invest in it.

Some of the 'consumerist' measures discussed here might help towards this end: in particular some fiscal changes, an increase in parental involvement in schools and their governing bodies, better quality of information from all educational institutions, better 'marketing' of post-statutory age opportunities, more investment from industry and a proper complaints system.

There is not a consumerist 'magic wand' that will transform the system, but there is a wind of change blowing against some of the old paternalist 'the service knows best' attitudes. The education world would be wise to espouse any idea – whether or not it is labelled 'consumerist' – which has a chance of improving performance in our weakest area – individual motivation – or which gives ordinary people a sense that they have some sort of control over their own educational destiny.

References

For a fuller discussion of education vouchers, see A. Sofer, 'School Vouchers – the Unanswered questions', *New Democrat*, September/October 1983.

For an account of the Cambridgeshire experiment, see Tyrell Burgess, 'Financial Self-management in Schools: the Cambridgeshire scheme', Working Papers on Institutions No. 53, October 1983, North East London Polytechnic.

Henney, A. *Inside Local Government*, Sinclair Browne, 1984, pp. 396–9.

Kegan, Johnson, Peckwood and Whittaker, *School Governing Bodies*, Heinemann Educational Books, 1984.

HMSO Government Green Paper, 'The Development of Higher Education into the 1980's', 1985.

NEDO/MSC, *Competence and Competition*, 1984.

'School Standards and Spending', Statistical Bulletin 13/84. DES.

Taylor Report, 'A New Partnership for our Schools', the Report of a Committee of
    Enquiry appointed by the Secretaries of State for Education and Science and for
    Wales, HMSO, 1977.

For a fuller account of the new procedures, see the Special Education Handbook issued
by the Advisory Centre for Education (ACE).

Heap, B., *Degree Course Offers 1986*, Careers Consultants, London, 1985.

'Improving Secondary Schools', (The Hargreaves Report), ILEA, 1984.

'Obtaining Better Value from Further Education', Adult Commission, 1985.

6 Health
David King

An assassin's bullet came close to killing the Pope in 1981 but his life was saved and the doctors found him a model patient. He made a good recovery and after a few days asked if he might attend the regular medical conference reviewing his condition and was made welcome. During the meeting he requested permission to speak which the doctors granted and he addressed them for half an hour on the subject of involving their patients more in decisions affecting them, listening to their point of view, sharing information, and taking their wishes into account when deciding on treatment. It seemed like a modern parable for it indicates how widespread is the feeling that people should be more involved in the management of their own health – it is not peculiar to this country or the NHS – but that they do not expect doctors and other health professionals to welcome the idea. If the Pope approaches the topic of consumerism with caution, lesser mortals have some excuse for diffidence.

One reason for this defensive attitude of professionals is that they have been trained always to act in the best interests of their patients. Florence Nightingale gives a good account of this view in her book (Nightingale, 1859). She appears to have sympathetically considered every aspect of the care of patients including how their privacy, dignity and morale could be maintained – it is as valuable a guide today as it was when written more than a hundred years ago. Every aspect of care seems to have been weighed except the patients' own views and wishes: it may be she believed that acting with their best interests in mind is as good or better than asking them what they want. This is consistent with her definition of a nurse as 'any person in charge of the personal health of another', suggesting that health is much too serious a matter to be entrusted to the individual. Now the nurses of Florence Nightingale's day were mostly domestic servants, so how much greater is the dominion of trained and qualified professionals over the patients in their charge. To be a patient is to resign oneself to the passive acceptance of all that those in charge of your personal health deem is in your best interests: to seek their help is to become a patient.

Whatever their grumbles, people have accepted this view and submitted to the mystery of medicine and the vagaries of the NHS: but in recent years there has been a noticeable change. It is too slight to describe as a fundamental shift and too persistent to dismiss as a passing aberration. It may stem from a growing realisation that ill-health can be encouraged by life-style: that illness is not always chance misfortune to be taken to an expert and put right: that you can take avoiding action. A good example of this change is the altered style of TV programmes which once had titles such as 'Your Life in Their Hands' – a privileged peep over the surgeon's shoulder – but today are called 'Well-Being' or 'Body Matters', whose message is much more, your life in your hands. Then there have been the well-reported instances of the fallibility of medical science and a growing realisation that drugs, vaccines and surgical procedures can do harm as well as good. Finally, there is a mood recognised by all political parties that people want more influence on the services provided for them. There has been the growth of pressure groups and self-help movements among people with a disease or condition in common, increasing evidence of a sympathetic response from some doctors and professionals to share information and responsibility with their patients, but most noticeably, the various structural changes to the NHS all intended to increase responsiveness to the needs of its customers.

In its first 26 years the NHS reflected the traditional view of health for it was a totally enclosed and secret institution. Within it there were the doctors ministering to their patients, and the administrators eking out the meagre resources: there was no opportunity for public participation or access to information about health policies or the management of health services. 1974 changed all that. The NHS was reorganised and exposed to public view with public meetings, public watchdogs, community health councils (CHCs), and published detailed plans of health authority intentions which required public approval before implementation. Great faith was placed on the idea that good planning and good management would produce the joint by-product of better services for patients. But the change in financial climate ruled out the type of planning people like best – planning to spend more money – and the management became muscle-bound because it had no common purpose. The public exposure was a massive shock, and health authorities have often reacted badly to CHCs who on remarkably slim resources have striven hard to represent the case for the consumer, though some seem only interested in scrapping with health authorities. Concern over the bureaucracy of the NHS and its remoteness from public opinion has led to two further reforms, the most recent in 1983 when Roy Griffiths reporting to the Secretary of State (Griffiths, 1983) saw greater responsiveness to public demand as the principal objective for the NHS. Resulting from this general managers have been appointed to concentrate attention on this theme and ministers review the service annually to ensure there is no deviation from the objectives they set.

Consumerism is not democratic or fair, there are no rules of the game as to who shall or shall not have influence: the most effective voice wins. That the wrong people are being consulted or listened to is a cause of much concern to some who challenge the legitimacy of representatives and question their motives. There are worries that the middle class, men, organised handicap groups, families and carers are simply joining the professionals' bandwagon, feathering their own nests and suppressing the voice of the real consumer. The other criticism is that authority selects its own representatives who will say what it wants to hear – tokenism.

It is possible to be in favour of consumerism without believing that consumers are always right and professionals invariably wrong, simply that they have some obligation to debate and reason with each other. William Inman (1985) makes the point that even with those drugs under active suspicion, 'the mortality rate is two or even more orders of magnitude, that is 100 or even 1000 times, LESS than the risk of dying from the disease'. He claims that 'trial by television' resulted in the removal of a drug from the market though there was only one death reported in the USA.

Sir Hermann Bondi writing in the same book states, 'as a citizen I would give up all the present teaching of mathematics if we could give people a little feeling for statistics and probability, for that is truly important for responsible citizenship'.

High quality medical care is the public's first requirement, but in addition to this people now want more influence on what happens to them and the way the health service is run. They want services designed for their convenience, closer to them and promptly available. Can the NHS deliver? The odd thing is that however intractable a problem may seem, there will be one or more places in the NHS where it has been cracked – the difficulty then becomes how to get others to apply the solution. I have selected five aspects of consumer interest to assess the prospects for change and improvement. Some offer promise but others seem to be as insoluble as ever, and none more so than the problem of delay which I turn to first.

If only there were an easy solution to the waiting game, the Achilles heel of the NHS. It is a strange enterprise which attracts more business but is expected to fulfil the extra orders on a fixed level of funds, yet that is the constraint on the NHS. Because there is no increase of income in step with the increase in output there is little incentive to review working budgets, for with no more cash to replenish them it only leads to frustration. There is a constant and fruitful search for improvements in productivity, though this is limited at times on grounds that it infringes clinical freedom. That patients, to avoid delay, can pay the same staff for private treatment is a financial disincentive to the eradication of waiting lists. The USA has no such problems about access to service because in general for every course of treatment a fee is paid by the government or private insurer and revenue increases with work. There the problem is how to limit ever-growing expenditure on health care, currently about twice that of the UK. Research reported in the *New England Medical Journal*, (August 1984) suggests that the considerable variation in hospitalisation rates in the United States is accounted for by the admission policies of individual doctors. Since there are vastly more people who could reasonably be admitted to hospital for treatment, government action to limit hospital revenues may lead to higher admission rates for those conditions which produce most profit. Getting a balance between what is medically necessary and what is affordable is a common problem and can only be understood and influenced by more and better informed public debate. It will be an interesting test of consumer pressures and the attitude of the NHS to them to see if this takes place.

Inability to cope with demands in excess of current capacity is something people may understand, but there is no defence for the delays and sometimes brusque response many experience once they are out of the queue and in the system. The NHS has recently appointed general managers, one of whose key tasks is the responsibility for improving customer relations and since the renewal of their contracts depends on improved performance, some changes can be anticipated.

One idea frequently explored to increase the potency of the individual consumer is to introduce the power of the purse either by giving consumers cash grants or tokens with which to buy services. There is nothing novel in this concept since there are already instances where the exercise of individual choice has direct financial consequence, notably in the selection of a general practitioner who is credited with a capitation fee for every patient enlisted. Although there is talk of competition among family doctors, little exists at present; there is nothing to enable the potential patient to assess the alternatives available, nor to indicate what services have been acquired once the decision is made. It is a financial transaction which gives minimal influence to the consumer. In theory, the consumer is free to change doctors and seek a second opinion, but in practice there is nothing to explain or encourage the practice. Many people feel that there is positive discouragement for it indicates a lack of confidence in an individual and that to give offence to one doctor can affect relationships and the outcome of future consultations with the whole local medical community.

Professor Alain Enthoven (1985) of Stanford University has recently reviewed the possibilities of using financial incentives to sharpen NHS performance. He proposes that district health authorities should regard the money allocated to them as annual premiums for the comprehensive health care of the people in their boundaries and use it to negotiate contracts with doctors to provide the type and quantity of services required. In brief, it envisages doctors in a contractual relationship with district health authorities. This is a long way from the current practice in which doctors do not see themselves managed in this way. Maybe the idea cannot be applied in this form, but it would not be unreasonable for the public to be told how much more service it can expect for any increased investment of resources.

Stripped of financial influence and the opportunity to shop around for service, the health consumer might expect some compensation in terms of rights and formal protection, but legal action and health authorities' complaints procedures are notoriously inadequate when things do go wrong.

Like many aspects of life in Britain, rights and legal responsibilities are ill-defined and in practice it is difficult to exercise them.

Financial mechanisms and formal procedures have their place and where they have not been effective, remedies should be found. The introduction of some competition among family doctors, encouraging consumers to shop around, could have a signal effect on other parts of the services.

When a doctor has been consulted, nothing can replace the account he or she gives to the patient and their discussion. It is information of the first importance for it is particular and personal. People most frequently complain about failures to keep them informed and it is an aspect of service for which doctors and health authorities should establish standards and review regularly. But people frequently want to know more about the condition which has been diagnosed than is possible in a relatively brief interview. They want to learn about the range of treatments and their possible effects, what they can do to help themselves, and often they want to hear from others who have been in the same position. There is considerable scope for information which supplements that which the doctor has time to impart or is possible for the patient to absorb in one sitting. Some years ago I visited a hospital in Oakland, California, which had just such an information centre to which doctors could refer their patients to learn more. There were many formats available: the printed word, audio-tapes, tape-slide explanations, discussion groups and lectures. It was an excellent way to ensure that information about health and ill-health was available.

There is currently an initiative in the NHS to give more prominence to health promotion and the Health Education Council and health authorities are working hard to improve this neglected area of activity. Publicity has not been one of the health service's great strengths and it may be more sensible to work in collaboration with specialists than try to develop its own skills for the public are used to the highest levels of quality in presentation. The College of Health, Gloucester and Exeter Health Authorities have jointly developed a telephone information service, 'Healthline', which has been introduced in three cities and could easily be extended throughout the country. Telephone enquirers can request information on some aspect of health or health services, and the operator selects the most appropriate of the nearly 200 recorded 4-minute tapes to play over the telephone. Its great advantages are that enquiries can be made anonymously, many people prefer the spoken word, it is rapidly available, and can be speedily updated. In another approach, the South Western Health Authority has worked with a professional agency to produce video cassettes to explain health matters to the public.

One important source of expert information is the experience of fellow sufferers to be found in the ever-expanding number of self-help groups for such conditions as asthma, multiple sclerosis and depression. People find it valuable to discover what improvement or relief others have found from orthodox and fringe medicine about which there is professional reticence or simply a lack of experience. The expertise of people who have made a special study of one condition may at times be better informed than that of doctors who only rarely encounter it.

People expect better information about the health service they pay for, its performance and how it is managed. There is increasing awareness of the markedly different levels of activity in various parts of the country, that services in some health authorities achieve far more than others with similar levels of resource. In a variety of ways this information is becoming available to the public. One example of this is the decision to publish reports of the Health Advisory Service and the National Development Team for Mentally Handicapped People. These are the bodies which examine and report on district mental health, mental handicap and geriatric services, they are the nearest we have to inspectorates and until now their reports were confidential.

Consumers can expect more and better information in the next few years, and if the NHS does not provide it, others will.

It is difficult to think of any policy more unpopular with consumers and more damaging to their interests than the wholesale centralisation which has been a feature of health as well as other public services in the past two decades. Closing what is conveniently local and agreeably small to form big distant units has been done in the name of better professional standards and the economies of scale but there is increasing evidence to challenge these assumptions from the variety of community solutions which abound. The development of local services is one area of consumer aspiration which promises to be easier to satisfy than others I have discussed.

I am not asserting that everything can be done locally, simply that more is centralised than needs to be. Ask the simple question: what is going to be done for this person that justifies a long journey from home? and you may decide that there are good reasons for centralising cardiac surgery, but less compelling ones in the case of care for the elderly. This often leads people to distinguish between 'care' and 'cure' services, the former being suitable for local provision but not the latter, they conclude that there is a once-for-all division which allows mental health, mental handicap, geriatric and primary care services to be local but that all others are best centred in district or regional hospitals. The matter is far more complex. There are many districts with local hospitals providing surgical services and consultant clinics in health centres: services which are undertaking appropriate work are popular and affordable. In the past it had been automatically assumed that they would one day be drawn into central hospitals, but why should such services not be extended to more localities? We accept that people with diabetes or kidney failure can care for themselves at home, handling drugs and carrying out complex procedures, yet in other instances these are the very reasons given for centralisation, that procedures are too skilled to be safely or economically dispersed. To illustrate the point that the picture can change there is the example of people suffering from cancer administering their own cytotoxic drugs at home. This is a recently introduced practice which until now was thought only possible as an in-patient procedure because of the toxicity of the drugs and the nursing skills required in their administration.

These are instances of things which may have been centralised for good reasons but which with experience can be localised: then there are services which should be local but either are never local enough or are perversely centralised. The classic examples are small clinic premises conveniently located which are replaced by big new inaccessible premises – a common inner-city problem: and communities wanting a branch surgery or pharmacy but who cannot make their voices heard – a chronic rural complaint. The dice are loaded in favour of centralised solutions; it requires far more proof to decentralise. But people prefer things to be local and the pendulum has swung too far in the other direction: so how is the NHS to be better rooted in the communities it serves?

Extend a principle which has already worked well and the answer may be within reach.

There are 14 health regions and have been since the formation of the NHS, it is only since 1974 that the regions were divided into districts which meant that there were defined populations, typically of 250,000 people, for whom services were planned and provided and who were to be consulted on health matters. Until the formation of districts the only influence on planning was professional interests and planners determined the location of services with scant regard to the convenience of the people served. The city in which I work possessed many examples of services for which people had to travel 40 miles and more from other parts of Devon, but since the formation of four separate districts in the county there has been a decentralisation from Exeter to neighbouring districts of chest medicine, opthalmology, mental health and mental handicap services much to the convenience of their populations. There has been similar experience of this kind of decentralisation in other parts of the country.

What has worked so well for district populations within regions may serve communities within districts also. There is no generally accepted method of dividing up the population of a health district and this may account for the inconvenient location of some services and unnecessary centralisation of others about which local communities complain. Remove an old person a long way from home and, however good the care, the lifeline of contact with remaining family and friends can easily be severed, yet long-stay care for the elderly is frequently distant from the localities served. There are 'drop-in' centres and short-stay care facilities so far from some of the people for whom they are intended that they cannot use them. If district health authorities were required to recognise and cater for the natural communities which exist within their boundaries there might be a better basis for planning and providing community services. In all the districts I have visited people have a good sense of their natural constituent localities but do not always take the next step of recognising them to plan service provision. In common with many other districts we in Exeter have experimented with ways of identifying the communities we serve and this has led us to something we call 'locality planning'. So far we have identified 12 localities where social, geographical and historical factors suggest a community: not local government boundaries, size of population or the usual determinants bureaucracies impose. The localities usually comprise a small town and the villages which look to it for schools and shops, they range in size from 10,000 to 40,000 people. There are similar community territories within cities too and although we have applied it to our small city, it would be interesting to see it working in a larger urban setting. The principal effect of 'locality planning' has been a greater degree of decentralisation than any of us had thought possible. Perhaps the most graphic example is that we are spreading from one big mental illness hospital, which has traditionally provided services for the confused elderly, to nine separate locations each with its residential, day care and visiting domiciliary services.

Having someone plan for you, however sympathetically, is no substitute for being consulted and participating in the debate yourself; better planning in the future must mean greater consumer involvement. There are two main aspects of participation, the first is discovering what people want and the second is getting an organisation to do something about it. Sampling consumer opinion is a relatively new activity for the NHS, but we can expect to hear much more of it. Ham (1985) has compiled a variety of examples where community health councils have collected consumer opinion and thereby influenced change. In Exeter we commissioned Professor Brimblecombe to find out from handicapped young adults what they want so that we can cater for them and his first report has recently been published (Brimblecombe, 1985) and is already informing our plans and services. Handicapped people and their families who have not previously received help cannot be expected to give precise specification of their requirements and the teasing out of what is wanted is an important new skill to be applied. Many districts maintain registers of handicapped people, another example of how consumer information is collected as a basis for service design. This approach is much more locally sensitive than what has served until now, the 'norm' – applying to your population the national average expectation. Collecting good local information should not be limited only to the time when new services are being planned but also to judge whether they are working as intended and still providing what customers require. There will be much more market research, consumer surveys and service evaluation in the future with reports publicly available.

Community health councils (CHCs) were set up to represent consumer interests to health authorities and with more emphasis on consumerism their spirits should be high, but morale appears to be low. The reasons for this include the fruitless mutual antagonism between some CHCs and health authorities, their inadequate resourcing (they usually have only the funds to employ a secretary and a clerical assistant), and a feeling that if health authorities become more consumer-conscious there will be no place for CHCs. However well disposed the NHS becomes to the consumer, it remains a monopoly and the consumer has no real alternative. This reason is sufficient to justify the retention and strengthening of CHCs. In recent years there has been a trend to include representatives of voluntary organisations and consumer interest groups on the planning teams which most health authorities have formed to design and review services. In the field of mental handicap this has enabled families who use the services to influence the debate. It is possible in some instances for consumers themselves to participate and in Hampshire, Derbyshire and Exeter there are Centres for Independent Living in which physically handicapped people are involved not just in an advisory capacity, but in the running of services. These are all examples of participation at the district level, but for most of us district is remote and isolated from daily life and being involved in activities at a much more local level is infinitely preferable.

In connection with the 'locality planning' ideas mentioned above, we have been experimenting with ways to increase local participation. A planning team has been set up for each locality and members include locally-based professionals from health and social services, and public representatives who live locally, usually elected councillors who have expressed an interest for the work is entirely voluntary. To avoid lay opinion being swamped, the CHC has established a number of health fora – mini-CHCs – to sample local opinion. In addition, parent members have been included in the joint health and social service mental handicap teams, which plan and manage the community service for each locality. These various initiatives have in common an attempt to make the interests of consumers uppermost. People understand their locality and its needs in a way that neither they nor professionals can comprehend a district. The most frequent NHS contact people have is with their family doctor and in a number of practices around the country, patient participation groups have been instituted enabling people to become more involved in their own health, the care of others and the operation of the practice they have joined. Health professionals say that such groups enable them to give a higher priority to prevention and redefine their relationships with their patients. Every encouragement should be given to the steady increase of such groups.

Most people approve of things the way they are, they like the health service and find no major fault in it, but a growing number consider it fails to treat them in a mature and adult fashion. They perceive a prescriptive, inflexible system which diagnoses and treats, expecting the patient meekly to accept, when what they want is to be consulted, listened to and given choice. There are many doctors, nurses and other professionals who agree with this, but not yet the majority. There are administrators who believe that scarcity of resources precludes all choices, other than Hobson's choice, and that pandering to the consumer can only unleash insatiable demand. If the change that some see as inevitable is not to be too painful, what can be done to adapt to it?

There are five areas in which action is required:

1. The climate of opinion created in the NHS which has put consumer affairs high on the agenda must be maintained. Without continued drive and encouragement from politicians it is not certain that NHS professional interests would afford it so high a priority.
2. Something must be done to restore the morale of CHCs and get relationships between them and health authorities working more effectively in the interests of consumers.
3. Though the areas of consumer rights and financial mechanisms have not been abundantly fruitful, they must not be ignored and fresh efforts should be made to increase their effectiveness.
4. It will be no surprise to the reader that I consider the single most important step to be taken next in making the NHS more user-friendly would be the general adoption of something like 'locality planning', dividing up districts into localities based on natural communities each with its own participative arrangements to involve consumer representatives in planning and service delivery.
5. To achieve all this will require training and development of staff, not just in improved public relations techniques, important though these may be, but in carefully changing old orthodoxies and attitudes.

The process of change will be gradual and not achieved in a few years, it can only be said that a start has been made. Michael Young, who founded the Consumer Association and the College of Health has recently written:

> Consumerism of any sort has one single characteristic which makes it anathema to some: it feeds on itself. The more people become aware of their own bodies, of the treatment for their ailments, of the workings of the health services, the more active they will become, and in some ways the more prickly unless their aspirations are respected'. (Young, 1985)

In the health sector, consumerism has fed on itself and people do want more of it, in this they have the support of all political parties: there is not much comfort for those who find it anathema and wish it would go away. In any case, can it be anathema if it has the support of the Pope?

References
Brimblecombe, F.S.W., *et al.*, *The Needs of Handicapped Young Adults*, Paediatric Research Unit, Royal Devon and Exeter Hospital, Exeter, 1985.
Enthoven, A.E., 'National Health Service: Some Reforms that Might Be Politically Feasible', *The Economist*, 22 June 1985.
Ham, C., 'Consumerism in the Health Service: State of the Art', *Health and Social Service Journal*, 30 May 1985.
Inman, W.H.W., 'Risks in Medical Intervention', in Cooper, M.G. (ed.), *Risk, Man-Made Hazards to Man*, Clarendon Press, Oxford, 1985.
NHS Management Enquiry, Letter to Secretary of State, DHSS, 6 October 1983.
Nightingale, Florence, *Notes on Nursing*, Dover Publications, Inc. New York, 1969.
Report on the First Year of Healthline, College of Health, 1985.
Wennberg, J.E., *et al.*, 'Will Payment Based on Diagnosis-Related Groups Control Hospital Costs?', *The New England Journal of Medicine*, vol. 311 no. 5, 2 August 1984.
Young, M., 'The Expectations of Patients', *The Medical Annual* (1985) 1 78-183.

7 Housing
Debbie Ounsted

This chapter looks at the role of consumers in that often ignored sphere of public policy – housing. Housing differs in many ways from the other services discussed in this book. Unlike health care, everyone needs housing continuously, all their lives. Unlike the home help service or education, housing is the individual's ultimate consumer durable. In theory one might expect more user involvement in the planning, delivery and management of housing than in other services. This chapter examines the degree of consumer involvement in many forms of housing tenure. It concludes that consumerism, irrespective of tenure, is only effective where the consumer has control over the resources needed to provide, manage and maintain the service.

Owner-occupation in Thatcher's Britain is the norm. Owning one's own home is undoubtedly a popular way to live. Home ownership has grown consistently over the last 50 years, irrespective of the party in power. Since 1979 the main thrust of government housing policy has been towards finding methods of encouraging more home-ownership opportunities for a wider range of people. A survey carried out for the Building Societies Association in March 1983 ('Housing Tenure', the Building Societies Association, 1983) shows that 62 per cent of all adults (as opposed to house-holds) were owner-occupiers, but that 78 per cent expected to be owner-occupiers within the next ten years. For people under 35 the demand for and expectation of council accommodation was virtually nil. There are no indications that any future government will take steps to reduce the trend.

It could be argued that home ownership is the ultimate way of providing consumer control in housing. In theory the householder both owns and can dispose of the property, and decides how it is run. However, there are contradictions. In theory a home owner has complete control over the maintenance of the property. In practice that control is not effective unless the home owner has the ability to identify and to know how to deal with defects, has the money to set problems to right, and the motivation to follow that maintenance through. Evidence of the problems inherent in consumer control in owner-occupied dwellings, is the growth of the 'staying put' schemes.

These projects have been set up to provide an advisory, financial and building service to elderly owner-occupiers who, while they may have a large financial stake in the property, lack the knowledge, motivation and the cash to keep the stock in good repair. The incidence of disrepair and lack of amenities in dwellings owned by elderly people, particularly in the cities, is remarkably high. Indeed the deterioration of the owner-occupied stock is increasing faster than that in other sectors. So it does not follow that ownership in itself enables the consumer to run his or her personal housing service properly.

Home ownership therefore does not necessarily bring with it the ideal of consumer control. Moreover, although a home owner may be able to make some decisions which a tenant cannot – for example, whether to do structural alterations – none the less there is no mechanism for influence over events that occur outside the dwelling. A home owner has no one but the police to complain to about noisy neighbours or dogs fouling the front lawn. Residents' Associations may spring up to campaign for improved service delivery, as Tenants' Associations may do on a local authority estate. However, they are unlikely – at least when they first emerge – to demand a role in planning the future housing service for future generations of occupiers. They are more likely to have only an immediate and localised concern for the quality of their own neighbourhood, today. However, where authority to make decisions on their own behalf is vested in Residents' Committees (for example, in blocks of leasehold flats, or in some cooperative ventures) the picture can change, but success will depend on the degree of commitment, and the amount of resources available to users. So effective consumer control is not an automatic corollary of ownership.

None the less, the Thatcher government, consistent with the belief in the value of consumerism, has laid great legislative store by home ownership. The right of council tenants and those of non-charitable housing associations to buy their own homes has not only become a statutory right, but is also encouraged by the fiscal mechanism of discounts. The ceiling for mortgage tax relief has been raised to £30,000, and whatever the Duke of Edinburgh may prefer, this looks likely to stay. For sitting tenants of charitable Housing Associations, a bizarre hybrid known as the HOTCHA scheme has been set up. This gives qualifying tenants the opportunity to get a discount to go away and buy a house on the private market somewhere else, thus freeing a rented home for another person in housing need. A number of new experiments to encourage owner-occupation have also been spawned. Shared ownership schemes, which many housing associations are now building, offer a tenure where the property is part owned and part rented by the person who lives in it, the costs being midway between those of a full home owner, and those of a full tenant. They take on the responsibility for day-to-day maintenance, but not structural repairs. There are a number of variations on this scheme. The shared ownership initiatives at least provide an opportunity for people who would not get a look in for publicly rented housing, because of their income level or their lack of housing need but who none the less cannot afford full owner occupation straight away. They are of particular use to young single people working in areas of high-cost housing. Leasehold schemes for the elderly which provide both an equity for the elderly person, and a level of caring service which the individual has to pay for, carries the tradition of sheltered housing through into the owner-occupied sector.

But ownership in itself does not mean that the consumer automatically takes a greater interest in influencing future housing policy. Indeed, it seems to be the case that significant dissatisfaction with existing services is the only spur to consumer involvement. Perhaps the same is true in other areas of social policy.

Where owner-occupied housing differs so fundamentally is that individuals have a real financial investment in it. Tenants by contrast have no direct financial reward for the amount of money they spend each week on housing. But it is not necessarily for investment purposes nor for consumer control that such a large proportion of Britons opt for owner-occupation. Many buy because it is the only way they can get housed, given the great shortage of acceptable public (and private) rented housing.

The Building Societies Association admits, at present, to some 30,000 serious mortgage arrear cases which will necessarily lead the building societies movement into a greater degree of property management than they have had in the past, and indeed than they may wish for. There is an irony in the fact that those who own homes have as little security if they fail on their mortgage repayments as do public sector tenants if they fail to pay their rent. Indeed, there is less likely to be the intercession of a sympathetic housing officer working on behalf of a home owner who has got into financial problems. Home owners who lose their jobs are only likely to have the interest element of their mortgage paid on their behalf, whereas a tenant may receive 100 per cent state assistance. Many former home owners will have had the bitter experience of having had their application for housing on the grounds that they have become a homeless family rejected by the local authority, who deem them to have made themselves homeless wilfully. Moreover, a home owner does not have the same statutory responsibilities of repair as a landlord does under section 32 of the Housing Act 1961.

As far as design and construction standards of new properties built specifically for owner-occupation, it is the market and not individual users who determine the standard. Recent criticisms of homes built by some modern developers indicate that the determining factor is the cost of construction plus the builders' profit element in relation to the aspirant buyer's willingness to pay. The NHBC provides a basic ten-year guarantee; but this compares poorly with the 60-year life required in the public sector for new house building. So it would seem that having a financial investment in one's housing does not automatically mean that it has been provided and will be run in the best possible way, even though the theoretical opportunity for complete control is there.

So is consumer involvement more highly developed in other tenures? In all sectors, but in particular the public rented sector, various methods of participatory planning and management have been set up, with varying degrees of success. Some housing associations have been in the forefront of attempts to give consumers a say in which services are provided. This has happened in different degrees and in varied ways. At Circle 33 Housing Trust, for example, a housing charity which has provided 5000 rented homes in north London, there has been since the late 1970s a major attempt to involve tenants in service provision. This was done first on a geographical basis as the Trust's work was split in four areas. In Camden (with the initiative coming from the paid staff, not from the tenants themselves) a series of meetings were held over a two-year period with tenants in different streets to encourage them to elect representatives to form a local area committee. The committee was carefully structured so that representatives from various parts of the borough could be elected, the number being in proportion to the number of tenants in the particular patch. Postal voting was held each year to elect nominated tenants, or votes in person were made at the Annual General Meeting. All tenants were automatically members of the Camden Area Association which thus elected the Camden Area Committee. The Committee comprised not only tenants' representatives but representatives from various designated local groups with an interest in the work of the trust (for example, the local Council for Community Relations, and the local Society for Mentally Handicapped People, in addition to a representative from the local authority and a staff member).

While the Trustees of Circle 33 centrally were not able legally to delegate all their decision-making powers and responsibilities to the area committees, the area associations were able to become corporate members of the Trust. In practice, the influence of the area committees over a whole range of issues was very important. The committees looked not just at issues of management and maintenance – for example, what maintenance response times should be, and how the trust was complying with its responsibilities to tenants under the 1980 Housing Act – but in a much wider sense looked at the Trust's development activities, and opportunities for new work in the borough. The flaw in the system was that it relied on the goodwill of the Trustees to listen to the voice of the area committees. A change in emphasis could easily have excluded tenants from the sphere of influence. Moreover, the need for education and training of tenants as participators cannot be too highly stressed. Consumers cannot effectively be involved in decision-making unless they are given time fully to understand and be given wide information about the complex issues involved.

On 30 per cent of housing association main committees there are now tenants. However, there are problems of tokenism. It is possible for a small number of tenants to be swamped by the professional committee members who may have different motivations for being involved in the committee work. Tenants may also find themselves in a difficult position as members of a main committee if their interest in day-to-day provision of services is not allowed a proper outlet by the majority of committee members. There is also a danger that tenant representatives end up getting sucked into seeing things only from the landlords' institutional point of view, leading to their effectiveness becoming neutralised.

Local councils by their nature cannot vest authority in their tenants (although tenants may be elected councillors). But they can, and many do, draw on representatives from tenants' groups to guide the formulation of housing policy locally. In Haringey, area committees, chaired by local councillors and comprising elected members, tenants and other interested parties, can exert significant influence on the Housing Committee about local issues. Whether this leads to better service provision only in the localities which have the most skilled advocates has yet to be studied. While such decentralisation can obviously create a more receptive environment in which consumers can influence debate, there can be problems of accountability both by tenants' representatives back to their patches, and of decentralised committees whose members are not all elected by the same constituency as the councillors to whom they report.

Much of the success of examples of consumer participation seems to rely extensively on the degree of willingness between the parties to work together, and a belief in the importance of participative relationships, this being more important than the formal structures.

An interesting example of a successful but loose participatory venture was that of the work carried out in Islington on the Hornsey Lane estate in the late 1970s. This was a pre-war estate of 202 dwellings in poor repair and was the council's first major attempt to involve consumers directly in improvement of their own living conditions. The council appointed the first estate action manager. This meant real decentralisation. An officer of the council was put in an office on the site with responsibility not only to control maintenance but much more importantly to coordinate the work of the various departments of the local authority and to work with the tenants' committee. The officer on site had power to order minor repairs. A liaison architect for longer-term repairs also worked on site and a number of major improvements were eventually put under way.

A new look at the lettings and management policy of the estate was also required. A special transfers policy was set up to enable some tenants to move out reducing the density on the scheme. In practice, this created some problems owing to an exodus of middle-aged couples. Vacancies created were let to young single people. The tenants' association became worried that too many new single people on the scheme would reduce stability. An imaginative policy of letting larger flats (which they would under-occupy) to young couples straight off the waiting list was set up, and this had the effect of reducing density while enabling tenants with a commitment to the future of the estate to move in.

With a combination of proper and effective maintenance, planning for future improvements and a positive management strategy, the estate was gradually transformed. Crime and vandalism plummeted as the child density reduced. There was better liaison with the police, and a creation of a sense of pride in the estate amongst the tenants. There is no doubt that the effectiveness of this approach had three key features. First, the tenants became well organised (although the number of people remaining actively involved was only about 15 per cent of households). The committee's chairwoman was politically astute. Secondly, it was the first such scheme in the borough and at member and officer level there was a strong commitment and sympathy with the aims of the tenants' association. This spread widely through local community groups, and inevitably led to a lot of individual interlinking. For example, the caretaker at the local community centre which was used by the tenants for their meetings was married to an active member of the local housing committee. Thirdly, the most important, and nowadays most difficult aspect, money, was available for the work that the tenants wanted to have done.

Other such schemes have been set up in many boroughs (for example, the Lea View estate improvement project in Hackney) and they seem to be an effective way forward.

The fullest and most effective method of involving people in their own housing is through the cooperative housing movement. There are a number of examples, and the cooperative movement is still expanding. A success story is that of the Weller Streets Cooperative in Liverpool which has recently won a Housing Centre Trust award. Here, a group of tenants took the initiative to work with professionals to plan their own new housing when the local authority threatened their existing homes with demolition. The coop had the energy and the initiative to stay together through a long process of what could have been community devastation. Residents had formed an action group in the late 1960s, but it was not until 1977 that setting up a housing coop was discussed at a public meeting. The coop used a development agency to help them get established, to acquire finance and land, and to design, develop and manage the estate which was subsequently built. Money was provided to build the housing scheme by the Housing Corporation.

Between the formal registration of the coop and occupation of the new houses, was a gap of 4 to 5 years. Such a delay required major commitment from both the prospective tenants and the professionals whom they appointed. Architects held about 100 evening meetings with groups of coop members, both about the overall proposals for the scheme and about individual houses. Coop members had put in an enormous amount of work, and particularly impressive is the fact that despite the original homes having been demolished, the coop held together, even though this meant for many people making journeys in the evening to get to meetings. (One member spent £250.00 on bus fares attending committees!)

One of the crucial elements of the success of this coop was the way in which the professionals worked with them to give them information to enable them to make choices. This included arranging visits to housing schemes, to the building centre, arranging slide shows, using overhead projections, models, videos and kits of small drawings. Coop members were able to gain a full understanding of the prospects for their future homes. It is the ability of members to make their own decisions which makes consumer involvement through coops so effective. In this instance, it was the members who decided what would be cut when the time came to look for savings in the tender. It was the tenants who decided they did not want their kitchens at the front, or thin plasterboard partitions. The architects could put their views forward but in the end would carry out what the coop decided. Interestingly, the architects themselves felt that participation at this level could prevent the problems that often occur when designing housing without consulting the clients first. They also concluded 'that a collective working-class client does not need any more education in design than any other type of client'. The Weller Streets Coop has decided to take over the management of its own houses entirely. The coop will continue to be responsible for collecting the rents, providing maintenance services, allocating properties and so on.

Cooperative housing must surely be the most effective method of individual clients being involved in the planning process. However, it must be remembered that this relates only to the properties in which they themselves will live. One interesting feature is that while planning laws and general legislation will prevent a coop from making any outrageous development decisions, the experience of the Weller Streets was that members were very clear about what they liked in design, and that was traditional approaches but with imaginative external materials.

At an individual level, public sector housing consumers are very rarely consulted about the design of their dwellings. An exception is the planning of adaptations, or a new property to suit the needs of a disabled household. There are many instances of housing associations, local authorities and indeed some of private builders working with disabled clients in order to provide customised design features. But this kind of detailed approach is not a possibility for most public sector landlords. They do not, in the main, know who their future tenants will be as housing allocations are done on the basis of who has the maximum housing need at the time that the property is produced. Moreover, what may suit one individual family may not be sensible in terms of longer-term housing management (for example, a particular family may as a matter of taste like to have open plan kitchen/sitting room, whereas the landlord may know from experience that the majority of households prefer to have these two rooms separate).

But despite these individual examples, the majority of tenants take little direct involvement in the planning of future housing or indeed in the running of the existing service. Success seems to be greatest when the initiative comes from tenants upwards rather than from authority downwards. None the less, there is one significant and interesting legal point. Secure public sector tenants must be the only consumers who actually have a right in law to be consulted about changes in the management of the properties in which they live. The Housing Act 1980 bought in the Tenants Charter. This is a fascinating piece of legislation as it gives to secure tenants a number of rights which a home owner would take for granted, for example the right to take in a lodger or to make improvements. The right to be consulted is the most interesting of these. Even the National Health Service only has to consult community health councils about major changes: and there is no duty to consult the individual users of the service.

Consultation does not necessarily mean that the person who takes the decision about the use of resources necessarily does what the person who has been consulted wants. None the less the intention quite clearly is to break down the traditional assumption that the person who owns the property is the person who calls the tune, rather than the person who lives in the property affected.

The Housing and Building Control Act 1983 intended to set the stage for further consumer choice by introducing the 'Right to Repair'. This sets a framework which will enable consumers of a maintenance service not to change it, but to opt to do the repair themselves, that is, opt out of using the service altogether. But the proposals are not as radical as they sound. They have been written from a landlord's eye view, and they do not so much give consumers a further right, as enable landlords to have the right to decide whether or not tenants *may* have the right to carry out their own repairs.

To sum up then, there are various structures already in existence for consumer involvement in housing in the public rented sector. That involvement is usually, but not necessarily, in relation to management and maintenance issues affecting existing housing schemes. In some instances both with local authorities and housing associations there are formal structures through which tenants can be involved. This may be on formal advisory panels or sub-committees. Full delegation cannot be granted by their controlling authorities to such bodies. None the less they can be valued highly for the part they play in bringing decision making closer to the people whom it affects.

Informal participative arrangements may be set up, often on a project-by-project basis. This may be to plan improvements on a particular estate or tackle management problems specifically associated with it. While the latter are more likely to stem from a direct demand by the consumers themselves who feel that taking some power into their own hands is the only way of achieving effective results, the former may well be established because liberal-minded people in authority believe that consumer involvement is a good thing in itself. In either case, some control over resources, and the availability of money and ideas to carry through programmes which show the results of action are a crucial part of success.

Cooperatives offer the best opportunity for consumer involvement in housing. But there is a need to consider some wider issues. The mutual cooperatives have the power to decide who gets housed.

Particularly given that public money is often involved, it is imperative that peer group control does not prevent the implementation of a fair housing policy. There is a danger inherent in cooperative structures that people with unfamiliar or unacceptable behaviour may be excluded from housing opportunities. The possibility of institutional racism is an obvious example. A second difficulty with the cooperative movement is the burden of voluntary work which it places on its members. While in theory all members may take an equal share in decision-making, in reality work may devolve on a few people. It is important that this work can be satisfactorily sustained over the long period of planning and building a new housing scheme and the eventual day-to-day management. Difficulties may occur when the glamorous challenge of planning a new development has to give way, once that has been satisfactorily achieved, to the routine but often difficult decisions which being a housing manager and a collective landlord imply. A coop will have to formulate a policy for action on rent arrears in the same way that any other landlord would have to do: but it can be more difficult to carry out what action may be necessary against someone who is a friend and neighbour.

In all instances where responsibility is devolved to consumers, and public funding is used, a proper accountability structure has to be established. This is not only to ensure that public funds continue to be used correctly, but also so that the delegating authority can obtain fresh information and ideas from what are likely to be the creative minds of consumers working together for their own benefit.

One major issue is unresolved. For the large number of those who have purchased the freehold interest in their property, they need consult no one about how they run their home. Equally, there is no opportunity for them to be involved in participatory structures with representatives of the people who financed and built their property. Given the clear benefit for future occupiers which arises from involving existing users in developing future housing schemes, consideration should be given to involving consumer representatives formally on professional housing groups, such as the Institute of Housing, on the policy groups of political parties at national and local level. The National House Building Council might benefit from having the experience of some first-time buyers at hand. The building societies, which finance the majority of house purchase in Britain today, will, in 1987, have power in law to build housing themselves. Perhaps they would be well advised to include some opportunities for owner-occupiers to be represented as a right on their boards.

So there are a number of ways in which individuals who use housing services can influence not only future design but also more significantly current management and maintenance policies. Secure tenants actually have a right to be consulted even if the right is a fairly slender one. Home owners, who in theory should be in the best position to take control, may only be so in practice if they have the information and the resources at their disposal to implement change: whereas tenants can have easier access to the professional services of the landlord or other advisors. Participatory methods can work, but only where there is an enormous willingness and a commitment on all sides, combined with available cash to get improvements carried out. The major difficulty about consumer involvement in housing is that while it is easy and appropriate for consumers to say what they feel is best for themselves, the issue becomes more complex when consumers are involved in making those decisions on behalf of other people: thus if you do not like the life-style or attitudes of the person coming to live next door, you may well take steps to prevent that from happening. Consumer control may not necessarily be compatible with equality of social opportunity.

References

Ash, Joan, 'Weller Streets Housing Cooperative', *Housing Review*, vol. 34, no. 4, 1984.
Boleat, Mark, *National Housing Finance Systems*, Croom Helm, 1985.
DOE, 'English House Condition Survey 1981', HMSO, December 1982.
'Housing Tenure', The Building Societies, 1983.
'The First Fifteen Years', Circle 33 Housing Trust, 1985.

For chief officers of local authorities, encounters with members offer some of the most frustrating and the most satisfying of work experiences. At this stage of my career it might be foolhardy to expand publicly on the former category, but an example of the latter may be quoted with impunity. New members of a Social Services Committee arrive with a refreshing ignorance of professional terminology and their questioning of the appropriateness of usages social workers take for granted often throws fresh light on otherwise accepted expressions. One such is the word *client*.

Accountants, solicitors and architects have clients. For social workers to have adopted the term is a token of their desire to transfer to the generally much more deprived users of their services some at least of the privileges associated with other older professions – the rights to confidentiality and to the undivided loyalty of the worker, and in general to the status afforded the recipient of a professional service. But for welfare service recipients these rights are by no means secure. Many social service clients are reluctant to become clients; indeed, became clients against their expressed preference. The social worker dealing with such a case is not single-minded in pursuit of the client's interest but is balancing this interest against those of other members of a family or group, may even be working against that interest on behalf of the employing body or another agency. This is not to criticise social workers, who have long recognised that social control must often be an aspect of their role, but it does suggest that practice betrays some of the aspirations inherent in the word *client* and may somewhat devalue its dignity in the process.

What are the alternatives? Terms which underline the client's role as a recipient of services, such as claimant or beneficiary, have the dual disadvantage of underscoring dependence and carrying with them the implication that the interaction involves the giving of cash, a benefit which in fact is rare in the personal social services. In health-related settings, *patient* is often used, though this fails to point up the crucial differences between medical and social work relations. In some areas of the social services a term can be appropriated from some other aspect of the client's relationship to the service; people in residential establishments are easily referred to as *residents*, and mothers and fathers in services focused on children are of course *parents*. But these cannot have general applicability.

In day centres and clubs, clients are often referred to as *members*, a valuable usage implying mutual support, some responsibility for the management of the group, a shared concern for the unit's programme, and the right perhaps to be involved in the admission or rejection of new members. The relationship between members and those who are employed on the club or centre's business is of course ambiguous. If a club decides to employ staff, to assist its honorary officers or to provide members with specialist services beyond the expertise they can muster among themselves, the staff are at least initially the servants of the membership, but their very permanence and knowledge gives such officials considerable power over time. In the social service setting in any case, the club or centre is not *owned* by the participating clients, so there are limits to the reality of the membership status.

Demonstrating at least partial dissatisfaction with all of these terms, some recent writers on the social services have looked for more precise or perhaps more neutral terms. Many have lighted on the term *user*, or more elegantly, *consumer*. To speak of consumers is to draw on a wide range of references, applicable to the provision of both goods and services. It does not pretentiously offer more than it delivers, since the power of consumers varies vastly between settings. A particular merit is that it focuses attention on demand, in a field in which the supply side has traditionally dominated the debate.

It has frequently been pointed out that the British political system is weighted heavily towards the interests of producers, the Labour Party historically representing labour and the Conservatives still powerfully identified with capital. Consumerism as a result has never found a regular home within these two major parties. Nevertheless the Right, at least in so far as it sees itself as the custodian of market freedom, is clearly more at home with the language of consumerism than is the Left with its commitment to the concepts of universalism, state initiative and fairness of provision. The Left's theoretical response to its distaste for the role of capital lies in nationalisation, profit-sharing and the cooperative movement. The Right, with little concern for egalitarianism, is free to concentrate on maximising the perceived advantages of market forces, using governmental power only to curb what it sees as the occasional, aberrant instances of malfunctioning. The total ideological picture is of course more complex than this, but it is important to acknowledge the political dimension to the debate over consumerism, in particular to understand why some sorts of proposals have made little headway among the makers of social policy.

It might be argued, for example, that a prerequisite of a market is purchasing power, a quality difficult to locate within most currently used models of social service provision. It is of course not true that all personal social services are provided free. Most residential services are charged, at least in part, to the users, in contrast with the health service, a situation which presents some anomalies. Domiciliary services generally have to be paid for when they involve practical help but not ironically when the help is professional. Social workers' time is given without payment; meals and transport often have to be paid for. The rationale seems historical and pragmatic rather than related to any principle.

In some service areas it would be very difficult to devise a charging system because of the difficulties of accounting for items of service, because a charge would discourage so many clients as to make the service pointless, or because clients have been in effect forced to accept services through court orders or similar. In the areas in which charges apply, however, consumers certainly enjoy some of the powers experienced on more open markets: those receiving meals could transfer their custom to cafés or restaurants or indeed prepare food for themselves; those receiving help with domestic work in their own homes could employ cleaners on their own account; those occupying places in residential establishments could transfer their custom to similar homes in the private sector. But payments for the purchase of service bring major disadvantages with them to services intended to promote public welfare, prevent more expensive future claims on public provision, and respond to the most acute needs. For these and other reasons many clients are not obliged themselves to meet the bills for the services they receive; charges are either rebated by the providing agency or subsidised or paid in full through the income maintenance system. The place of purchasing power in influencing the decisions of service planners and providers is thus severely curtailed.

This dilemma has provoked some thought among social policy theorists about substituting other media for cash in the purchasing process. There has been a good deal of discussion about, for example, the issuing of vouchers for the parents of school children. In the political context of the discussion, such schemes have usually been presented as a deliberate threat to schools perceived as less attractive and thus forced out of business. They have foundered, however, on the lack of easy adaptability on the supply side. Inescapably, to offer a range of choice involves the under-use of some facilities for at least some of the time, and the capacity to allow demand to switch between establishments and perhaps switch back again – a costly business.

In the social welfare field, the idea of social credits has recently been advanced, particularly in relation to the shift of some services with matching resources from the NHS to local authorities, but detailed feasibility studies have not been carried out over a substantial range of services. It *is* possible, however, to experiment on a small scale, particularly in areas of provision where services are still being set up, so that flexibility can be built in from the start. The parents of handicapped children, for example, could be issued with tickets to an agreed value with which to purchase from the issuing local authority, and perhaps also from local private and voluntary bodies, packages of service – day care, foster placements, short-term respite and so on – to suit their own needs. The limitations to the available provision is acknowledged in the total number of tickets produced, and the differential needs of different families are scored through their varied ticket allocations. Waste can be minimised as service providers become more skilled at anticipating demand and the feedback on relatively unpopular services is graphically quantified. In short, many of the advantages which accompany the operation of purchasing power in an open market can be reasonably efficiently replicated.

It is sometimes wrongly assumed that consumer choice depends on a system which embraces purchasing, but this is not so. Education departments often offer some choice of schools, and an NHS patient is free within certain limits to choose a GP and for certain conditions a hospital for in- or out-patient treatment. Social services operate for most services to stricter catchment areas, and since services are in large part funded it is natural that authorities should wish to serve predominantly residents in their own areas. Within the boundaries of social services departments, however, more could perhaps be done to extend consumer choice. Candidates for residential care are not always encouraged to express a view as to which establishment they would like to live in, nor are they provided with the information on which an informed choice could be made. For many other sorts of provision, departments have more than one establishment and could allow clients to select according to their own preferences rather than by departmental criteria. Day nurseries, home helps, training centres, even area offices need not be allocated only by geographical area but could provide opportunities for clients to choose whichever suited them best, even if their choices were odd or idiosyncratic.

The range of choice on offer is much broadened when the private and voluntary sectors are taken into account. Commercial organisations are naturally limited to areas in which profits can be made; there is therefore little private provision outside residential care and day care for the under-fives. Voluntary organisations by contrast often have independent sources of funds – accumulated capital, established voluntary fund-raising and grants from governmental bodies. Despite their often repeated claim to be the major source of innovation, voluntary organisations seem to have been reluctant to exploit the potential of their special status to provide alternative welfare systems. In the field of residential child care, for example, the large denominational organisations could together provide a wide range of choice. Instead, they have chosen to specialise into small areas of work, offering their residential places only to children already in local authority care. Significantly, this rationalisation is often presented as responsible coordination, ensuring that facilities are not duplicated; the implication seems to be that the public willingly accept a state monopoly of reception into care arrangements and would not any longer support the more diverse system which existed as recently as the 1960s.

Those who argue for social credits dispute this assumption and would urge voluntary organisations to be more bold in extending the public enthusiasm for choice in consumer goods into the field of welfare services. It is freely acknowledged that such a market would require a degree of regulation, a task which would naturally be undertaken by statutory bodies though not necessarily those which were themselves offering services and competing for custom. Many clients would need help in selecting for themselves the best possibilities from the range of services on offer; such consultation could be provided by knowledgeable *advocates* whose skill would lie less in their ability to offer a counselling service in their own right than in their wise guidance to the facilities available from other agencies. Organisations providing services would also need to be licensed and regularly inspected, to ensure that standards were maintained and that the whole range of provision were available in any given area – again a role for the statutory regulating body.

It is easy to be enthusiastic about markets when selecting only the points which work in favour of the consumer, but markets can also feature monopolies, sharp practice, exploitation and shoddy goods. Consumers of the social services are an inherently vulnerable group. They are likely if the market flourishes, to need a good deal of protection from commercial suppliers of services whose attitudes might be expected to be at least somewhat infected by motives of profit and the cut-throat conventions of competition. Social services departments already undertake some of the functions of regulatory agencies – inspecting private and voluntary residential homes, registering child minders, grant-aiding and contracting work to a range of voluntary organisations. Such quasi-entrepreneurial functions will grow substantially in the future if present trends towards greater diversity of welfare provision continue.

The commercial sector may also have lessons to teach statutory bodies about the running of their own services. British social services, for example, have traditionally taken a fairly passive attitude towards the promotion to potential consumers of what they have to offer, often of course because resource constraints have forced them if not actually to suppress demand then at least not to stimulate it unduly. As a result the most ambitious advertising work on behalf of social services has been carried out either in fields where social services departments were in effect promoting demand for other public sector services, as in welfare rights campaigns, or in drawing in additional resources in the form of volunteers and foster parents.

Advertising for foster and adoptive parents over recent years demonstrates how social service agencies can adapt their practice to the sharper demands of the quasi-commercial world. Bland general calls for families willing to take in an extra child were gradually supplemented by copy describing individual children, given false names to preserve anonymity up to the stage of an introduction. These in turn proved insufficiently individualised for putting across the needs of many difficult-to-place children and young people and, not without considerable professional hesitation, real, named candidates were presented, with photographs and even video-filmed personal appeals. Agencies which have used such approaches have certainly succeeded in recruiting families who would not apparently have been reached by other means, though as with other sorts of advertising the novelty may wear off and need to be replaced with fresh presentational devices. From a consumer perspective, the process has had an interesting side-effect. Advertising identifiable children has required their active cooperation in the preparation of publicity material and inevitably some frank discussion of the strengths and weaknesses of their selling points, an important step towards more honest participative social work with a difficult client group.

It may be that the marketing expertise which has been developed to supplement the resource side of the social service operation will in due course be used also to stimulate stronger pressure on the demand side. Lacking in most areas the potential to promote profits through increased take-up, social services managers are often at best ambivalent, at worst definitely fearful, of directly advertising the availability of services to unreached consumers. (As a result very little is known about the pre-client careers of either those who eventually become clients or those who fail to approach agencies; the contrast with the commercial sector's eagerness for knowledge about potential consumers of products and its substantial success in tracking down such information through market research is instructive.) But if the claims of social workers and others about the efficiency of their preventive work is to be believed, the stronger promotion of, for example, intermediate treatment for pre-delinquents, family casework for parents at risk of battering their children, and domiciliary services for elderly people likely if not given help to be candidates for residential care should actually save money by lowering the demand for the more expensive services which need to be brought into play if prevention fails.

The analogy with health education, whose advocates often face similar scepticism about the cost-effectiveness of their campaigns, is obvious. Clearly the links between good prevention or early intervention and later savings achieved through a lowered demand for emergency or long-term help has not been altogether persuasively made in the personal social service field. Hopes for a major extension of the use of advertising in stimulating social service demand may hang on the more effective arguing of that case.

There is one other field in which social workers have borrowed from the business world in recent years – the growth of the concept of a contract between a worker and a client. Some social workers now draw up, write down and sign contracts with their clients, with the acknowledged intention of specifying what the agency will and will not provide and what the client for his or her part will have to contribute to the bargain. This method of setting goals, prescribing limits and establishing a time-scale may be particularly useful in dealing with adolescents and their families where traditional rights and expectations have been undermined by changes in public attitudes but where the sense of fairness, mutual obligation and sanctions for non-compliance remain real and strong. Such contracts of course also define the obligations of the worker and the organisation providing the service and more particularly the limits to their rights which they accept in return for guarantees from the client. The existence of a contract clearly checks the power of the professional and goes some way to answering the argument that social workers' clients may be open to quite arbitrary shifts in the terms of their relationships with their workers.

Social service contracts of this sort do not of course have legal power but they are recognised as solemn and binding and since signatures are exchanged there is no reason why a client could not seek redress if an agency failed to honour its obligations. If, for example, a committee of a local authority reneged on the terms of an agreement made between a social worker and a client (it is not difficult to imagine such a situation arising in a case of a multiple problem family with rent arrears where the contract included a commitment to regular repayment of the debt) the client would clearly have a sound moral case, perhaps even a case in law. Short of such litigation the potential of contracts in extending the rights of consumers is certainly interesting. A clearer definition of the rights of those entering residential establishments, which at present fall seriously short of those of tenants in housing accommodation despite the obvious similarities of the service provided, is long overdue.

Many advocates of consumers' rights, in fields other than the personal social services, assume that substantial progress will only be made as a result of legislative change. In the fields of mental health and child care over recent years the legal rights of patients, parents and to some extent children have certainly been extended, though the general effect of such shifts is controversial. The legal enforcement of rights inevitably involves frequent recourse to the courts where the interests of the lawyers, the conventions of adversarial process and the complexities of representation seem often to distract from the more immediate interests of clients. Social work clients are often involved in conflicts of great complexity and the interests of several clients in a single case may differ markedly; litigation, particularly in family affairs, often seems more to formalise inter-client rivalries than to strengthen the client's position *vis-à-vis* the agency. Even when the interested parties to an action are a client on one side and an official body on the other, the courts usually provide a demanding if not actively unsympathetic environment for the client. The costs of legal action can be high, the risks of losing a case through inadequate presentation or technical deficiency are ever-present, and the problems of proving a shortfall in professional practice where standards are notoriously subjective and rarely amenable on the precise definitions and distinctions of the law – all these factors combine with the low level of confidence and bureaucratic adeptness of many clients to make legal action a rarely relevant recourse.

Some of the same objections to extending and formalising consumer rights in social service settings can be marshalled against a range of formal administrative measures involving quasi-legal procedures. Mechanisms for appealing against individual workers' actions or judgements, arrangements for considering complaints and offering redress, the operation of the ombudsman and similar officials seem often to ignore the fact that such professional and bureaucratic processes are fundamentally foreign to the working-class life-styles of most clients. Nevertheless the potential of administrative change in extending consumers' rights should not be underestimated. Moves to allow the clients of social services departments to see their own records may have led to relatively few formal requests for access, but the effect on social work recording and on social work practice must have been to add to the dignity of clients in seeking and receiving service.

The relative powerlessness of clients, both absolutely in society as a whole and relative to the organisations from whom they have to request help must be a starting point to the debate. Clients are not likely as a group to muster sufficient strength substantially to assert their rights as consumers. Significant adjustments to this imbalance of power will therefore only take place if social service agencies, their managers and the practitioners who work in them voluntarily surrender the rights over clients with which traditional practice has endowed them. It would be easy to be cynical about the hopes for such a development, but revolutions take place as often through the abdication of the powerful, or at least from their loss of will to hold on to power, as from the gathering might of the previously dispossessed. It is true that moves to open social service records were precipitated by the persistence of a client, Graham Gaskin, but little progress would have been made without the apparently self-destructive compliance of Liverpool City Council, the DHSS and the managers of social services departments who set up open access procedures. In short, the holders of political and professional power recognised the rightness – or perhaps the inevitability – of greater consumer power and moved deliberately to institutionalise these attitudinal changes.

Could it be that the semi-profession of social work is turning its back on the example of the older professions like medicine on which it had seemed to be modelling itself and taking a lead instead from the consumer movement? It would be too early to predict with certainty, and indeed the choice is by no means as stark as that contrast would suggest. But there are real signs, not only in Britain, that social workers are seeking more participative forms of practice as at least a counterweight to the paternalistic attitudes so often evidenced in the way doctors, lawyers and others deal with their customers. The British Association of Social Workers produced a report with the provocative title 'Clients are Fellow Citizens' early in the 1970s. Since then, the presence of clients at case reviews, the fostering of self-determination in clients in residential settings, the involvement of those attending day centres in the programming of activities, and many similar small but significant changes in professional procedures have contributed to changes in the nature of social service practice which might retrospectively be seen as decisive pointers to a major cultural shift.

The growth within the personal social services of attitudes originating within the consumer movement should not, however, be appreciated solely at the level of individual practice. The debate about consumer participation in the planning and management of services has a longer history, to be traced indeed through debate on the nature of democracy itself. Participative forms of government have always had as their objective the involvement of the consumers of services in decisions about the form services should take, but it would be naive to assume that any structure could easily embrace the wide diversity of interests which may be represented among an electorate. Local authority members may be distant in both their personal experience and their political attitude from the clients for whom the services they direct are at least theoretically designed. It is for this reason that the concept of plural democracy, with a much more diverse pattern of accountability for decision-taking, has found favour among those devising structures for the government of organisations providing social services.

Local authorities, which provide the greater part of Britain's personal social services through social services departments, have peculiarly direct accountability to the residents of their areas through ward councillors, each elected for a defined geographical constituency. The very strength of their mandate, however, should make them sensitive to alternative channels for representing the views of consumers, though the structures through which such views can be expressed are only fragmentary. The Barclay Committee proposed local welfare committees but where these were tried they had only very limited success. School governing bodies and community health councils have been suggested as models which social service authorities might imitate but neither seems altogether appropriate. Social services departments have no structure of decentralised units in any way similar to schools, nor any group who could so appropriately express a consumer viewpoint as parents. Community health councils on the other hand gain their strength from the very lack of local mandate in health authorities. It seems that a much more complex pattern of consultation is required if the consumers of social services, a group more diverse in their needs than the beneficiaries of either health or education services, are to have a direct say in how services are run.

The managers of services have to be preoccupied with supply-side problems, in effect with the rationing of resources, since outside the small commercial social service sector there is no balancing equivalent of demand and supply. The importance of consumers to planning is therefore that they are unequivocally able to express the voice of demand. It is a worrying feature that so few voluntary organisations have seriously concerned themselves with ensuring that the views of their consumers are adequately represented in decision-taking. Voluntary bodies are very varied in their management structures, governed often by oligarchies with only the most tenuous lines of accountability even to their sources of funds. With their professed record for innovation, some voluntary organisations at least could be much bolder in experimenting with structures which would give their clients opportunities to participate in policy making and planning.

In default of formal structures, both statutory and non-governmental organisations fall back on the sensitivity and alertness of their managers to the voice of consumers wherever it can be heard. Social service consumers are of course handicapped by their relative inarticulateness, and views will often have to be gathered at second hand through the experience of practitioners. Where an organisation has been formed based solely on the experience of clienthood, such as the National Association of Young People in Care, the problems of organisation, transient membership and long lines of communication have limited the impact which might otherwise have been made. Probably of more lasting significance is the contribution of those close to consumers, the parents, relatives, carers, foster parents and ex-consumers, who when organised into pressure groups can express views and provide feedback on services from a distinctively different perspective from that of the providing organisation. Of course, their position is also different from that of the clients themselves, sometimes very different indeed; the parents of the mentally handicapped, the children of the dependent elderly, the spouses of disabled people have needs allied to but distinctively separate from what might be called the primary consumers in such cases.

Managers of social services will be wise to look on pressure from such groups as a valuable source of data in the planning of services, and planning systems must allow space for this sort of input. In the statutory service the joint care planning teams and joint consultative committees established between health and local authorities provide a natural forum for the involvement of the voluntary organisations which are most likely to be able to speak with more or less direct experience of the impact of services on consumers. But other less formal channels are also valuable. Planners should make opportunities for meeting clients and hearing their point of view, by visiting establishments, by setting up groups of clients whenever appropriate, by listening carefully and sensitively on every possible occasion. Rational planning models make little allowance for such informal feedback on performance, alloting a tightly defined role to public or consumer consultation usually at a stage of the planning cycle where proposals have already been substantially formulated. Incremental systems are inherently more flexible, permitting, indeed encouraging, *ad hoc* input at every stage of the planning process and legitimising precisely the sort of back-tracking, gradual modification or unashamed reversals which need to characterise the apparently meandering progress of the really sensitive planner.

What hope is there then in the personal social services for a radical extension of consumer rights to a point at which it would be meaningful to speak of consumer power? It would be foolish to look for revolutions, but, as the process of providing access to records is demonstrating, substantial changes in both the attitudes and the practice of social workers can be achieved, sometimes quite quickly. Areas in which further progress might reasonably be expected in the short term include more regular consultation with residents in establishments over closure plans, modifications to buildings, redecoration and refurnishing, the involvement of clients of both residential and day care establishments in staff appointments, and the better promotion of arrangements for making and pursuing complaints. In all of these areas, greater consumer self-determination would run hand in hand with already established practices of encouraging better self-care and defending clients against institutionalisation. Where statutory bodies are considering privatisation, cooperatives of clients or, perhaps more realistically, of their relatives or carers, should certainly not be ruled out.

British social services, private, voluntary or statutory, have grown up on a model which depends largely on benign professional practice, but one important sector of service draws on quite different principles. The self-help movement appeals not to paternalism, charity and official outside aid, but to the knowledge, experience and zeal of those who have suffered, to help fellow sufferers. The process is less one of self-help than of mutual help, or as it has been described in a neat phrase, of serial reciprocity. The recovering addict uses his strength and insight to support colleagues at a more acute point of the cycle of suffering. The parent who knows what it was to harm her child recalls the mechanisms she discovered then to help others at risk of inflicting violence in gaining control of their feelings. The ideology is similar to that of the cooperative, both sorts of organisation sharing the sense of consumer solidarity.

To hope comprehensively to restore to conventional social services the vigorous reciprocity of the self-help movement is perhaps an idle dream. But it could be an important element in a campaign towards the recognition that consumers of social services have rights, dignity and indeed strengths of which conventional practice has often served to rob them.

Part III
Welfare in Practice

Introduction

So far in this book we have attempted to clad our framework of welfare consumers with more detailed analysis of the various structures of a consumer-oriented approach to welfare. Part II attempts to show how such an approach could be developed within a wide range of welfare agencies. Part III addresses the question of what such an approach would mean in terms of change of practices.

In Part III we have therefore provided some practical examples of services that we believe provide insights into the positive and also problematic elements of schemes that we believe exemplify some of the philosophies underpinning our notion of consumerism.

A common concern is the evaluation of new projects and the difficulties that project managers and operational staff have in stepping back and attempting to review programmes they have been involved in. On occasions this problem is recognised and objective analytical monitoring and evaluation processes are set up, usually through the involvement of external academic research workers.

Such a variety and corresponding variation in the quality of reviews is reflected in the chapters of this section. Although some are embedded in a rigorous academic study of schemes, others are based on the experience of project managers and although therefore they cannot be objectively neutral they do benefit from the knowledge and experience gained from being heavily committed to a new service.

Although each chapter considers a specific scheme, all of the authors have utilised the conceptual framework provided by the authors. Essentially the projects may be divided into three aspects. First, there are those schemes where consumers have been systematically involved in actually running services. Secondly, there are schemes which have created opportunities for consumers actually to develop informal choices in the sort of service they received. Finally, there are schemes where the notion of client/consumer rights have been placed at the forefront of the project's aims.

The projects that have been chosen exemplify at least one of these threads, although they are not exclusive. Whilst each chapter has a descriptive element which is specific to that scheme, all of the contributors critically appraise the success of the project and what features are useful lessons to those following on.

As we have stated earlier, there is a long lead-in time between ideas becoming policy options and such policy options percolating into actual services. The exposure of the successes and failures of these schemes will provide firm footing for those attempting to tread the path to a newer more sensitive and participative welfare democracy.

9 Case Management and Consumer Choice: 'The Kent Community Care Scheme'
David Challis

As consumers of social services, elderly people appear to be the most likely to respond positively when questioned about the quality of services provided (Rees and Wallace, 1982). However, since the expectations which elderly people have of services are frequently unclear (McKay *et al.*, 1973), this reported satisfaction must, in all probability, be seen as that of the contented recipient rather than that of the discriminating consumer. This pattern of acceptance by elderly clients was noted in one US study which was critical of the role of professional allocators since eligibility for and receipt of services are the prerogative of service providers whose assessments are not standardised but vary according to individual differences (Frankfather *et al.*, 1981). These authors concluded that the only way of achieving greater responsiveness to consumer preferences would be to replace individualised assessment and to eliminate flexibility and discretion by means of a service claim model, where users could select services by shopping among providers, and eligibility for levels of service would be determined by standardised assessments of disability. This is a modified social care market approach which aims to establish a degree of consumer sovereignty. However, there are important obstacles which render difficult the exercise of greater consumer choice by frail elderly people, whether in the current pattern of provision or with the market approach. These can be understood as first, characteristics of elderly people themselves and secondly, aspects of the service system.

Many elderly clients are not in the position to make optimal decisions alone or to exercise freely choice about care services. Physical and mental restrictions arising from disability associated with ageing combine with declining social resources to limit their access to knowledge and information which would enable them to make appropriate decisions. Carers similarly are frequently too concerned with the daily routine of care to acquire information and coordinate care without great cost to them in lost time. Secondly, the wide variety of types of need and times at which help is required do not readily correspond to the relatively inflexible and small range of services available. Individual services may well only contribute in a very partial way to the level of over all need. For example, domestic care may be available in the absence of more immediate personal care needs (Goldberg and Connelly, 1982; Wade *et al.*, 1983) reflecting the relatively small amount of resources devoted to the personal care tasks required by the very frail and vulnerable (Howell *et al.*, 1979). Such an inflexible, and often unpredictably partial scope of provision either leaves a client to endure a lower quality of life where service is absent, or more often, places the burden upon family and informal carers. Not only is the scope of coverage partial but the services which exist are organisationally fragmented since they come from a wide range of sources. These include different sections of the social services department and the health service as well as informal and voluntary sources. From the vantage point of the individual frail elderly client, the provision of care can appear all too often to be that of a series of piecemeal contributions by a range of different services, none of whom has an unambiguous responsibility for considering the wider ranges of need beyond their particular remit. Assessments and care plans tend therefore to be 'service-oriented' rather than 'client-centred'. Such a 'welfare-tray' approach (Goldberg and Connelly, 1982) will inevitably attempt to fit clients' problems into available, preordained service categories which are unlikely to be sensitive to a wide variety of needs and preferences. Thus, even the most well-organised provision of an individual service, considered in relative isolation to others, may, in relation to the over all spectrum of need, appear less than fully effective and an inefficient deployment of resources. Hence services have been not unreasonably described as 'an uncoordinated set of discrete and relatively autonomous parts' and 'the care which any individual old person receives is to a major extent fortuitous' (Plank, 1977, p.12).

Two factors have been identified which inhibit the capacity of frail elderly people and their carers to act as consumers in a social care market. The first of these is lack of information and the capacity to utilise it; and the second, market imperfections in the service system itself. Indeed, the greater the 'perfection' of the market from the point of view of economic theory, with large numbers of service providers none of whom is dominant, the greater the problem of organisational fragmentation. Thus, the cost of pluralism is an increasing need for effective coordination of provision both for elderly people and their carers. Other factors which can render a market solution an ineffective mechanism for greater satisfaction of consumer preferences or efficient use of resources include the unequal distribution of needs and resources and the presence of 'externalities' or important side-effects not taken into account by the market. These are discussed in further detail in Knapp (1984). If a consumer market-based approach to care is unsuitable, criticisms have been voiced equally of the failure of the professional approach to be sufficiently responsive to the preferences of clients. Indeed, a review of care services in the UK observed that a common problem has been 'the care-givers' failure to share explicitly with potential clients the aims and content of the social care proposed and, wherever possible, to obtain agreement to those plans' (Goldberg and Connelly, 1982, p. 54).

However, even those highly critical of the professional approach have recognised the importance of some retained discretion, particularly for those elderly people who are severely disabled and lacking family carers (Frankfather *et al.*, 1981). Others have indicated that informal carers too can benefit from information and assistance in planning and coordination of care (Greengross, 1981; Levin, 1982; Glendenning, 1984; Krulik and Hirschfeld, 1985). Social work in particular has been criticised on a number of occasions for working to differing agendas to those of clients of the service (Mayer and Timms, 1970; Ree, 1978), although the lessons of short-term contract-based approaches (Reid and Shyne, 1969; Goldberg *et al.*, 1985) indicate ways in which more effective help can be given where there is clear agreement between client and professional of both the objectives of help and the means chosen to achieve them. A review of recent studies confirms this. 'What is to be done and what is to be gained from doing it are clearly explicated and the client is engaged as a voluntary collaborator. Within this nexus are apparently potent ingredients for bringing about change' (Reid and Hanrahan, 1981, pp. 17–18). Herein lies the basis for a resolution of the professional approach.

The values underlying contract-based approaches to social work have much in common with the 'normalisation' principles which have been a popular recent development in long-term care. Wolfensberger (1980) has defined normalisation as 'Utilisation of means which are as culturally normative as possible, in order to establish, enable, or support behaviours, appearances and interpretations which are as culturally normative as possible' (p.80) for persons who are currently devalued. The value of the concept is that around it cohere a series of principles which have been relatively longstanding elements of good care practice. Amongst these relevant to our current concern are a belief in the individuality of clients, their right and need to exercise choice and control their own lives and the requirement that effective services are those which commence with a client's definition of the problem. The implement-ation of these principles in service provision provides a means to reconcile the consumer approach and the professional approach at the individual level by shared decision-making in the definition of problems and the formulation of care plans. The community care schemes are an attempt to provide a framework for care provision which can make this attainable.

The Basis of the Community Care Approach
The community care schemes were designed to provide care at home, where this was their choice, for frail elderly people who would otherwise require institutional care. The scheme was designed to achieve better use of resources by improving the effectiveness and ingenuity of social workers in the provision of reliable packages of care for frail elderly people. This involved devolution of the control of resources, by means of individual client budgets, to fieldworkers with responsibility for relatively small caseloads. The approach was based on the recognition that integrated care neither occurs spontaneously nor simply from improving the individual services which are

the components of a care package. Networks of care, sensitive to individual variations in need and preferences, were to be constructed and maintained by a key worker or 'case manager'. Thus the role of the social worker was to construct and maintain a coordinated package of care unique to each elderly person from a wide range of sources which are usually independent of each other: health, social services, voluntary and informal care. The work setting was modified in a number of ways to make possible the required changes from what has been the more usual practice in social work with elderly people (Stevenson and Parsloe, 1978; Goldberg and Warburton, 1979). The approach is detailed below.

Focused Care

The scheme was clearly targeted upon a high-need group. They were to be those elderly people whose needs were such as to place them at least on the margin of admission to a residential home. In the original project, a small team of three social workers covered the same district as a generic area team.

Smaller Caseloads and more Experienced Staff

Large caseloads are a commonplace in work with elderly people, but the staff in the scheme were to have caseloads of a size not dissimilar to those for people working with vulnerable children. This was designed to enable them to relate more effectively to the elderly person and their network, undertake careful and continuing assessment and monitoring of needs, liaise with other agencies and invest time and effort in raising community resources such as boarding out or neighbourly help. Continuity of responsibility and specialisation in work with a particular client group were designed to make possible greater knowledge of client needs, possible solutions and the range of relevant community resources. The staff themselves were expected to be qualified and more experienced than is frequently observed in the care of elderly people. Too often it has been noted that large caseloads of elderly people are managed by inexperienced or unqualified staff (Stevenson and Parsloe, 1978; Goldberg and Warburton, 1979).

Decentralised Budgets

Flexible responses to a variety of needs, represented by individually tailored packages of care, were a central feature of the scheme. To extend the range of possible solutions available to them the staff had control of a decentralised budget. All the expenditure from the social services department such as meals-on-wheels or home help was notionally charged to the budget, as well as actual additional expenditure upon new services or community resources. Hence an awareness of the unit costs of different services and alternative ways of meeting need was brought into fieldworkers' decision-making. Normally, by contrast, the only cost which fieldworkers can directly allocate, and consider in opportunity cost terms, is their own time. In order to provide a balance between this new greater autonomy in resource-allocation and the needs of an accountable agency, expenditure upon individual cases was limited to two-thirds of the cost of a place in a residential home, additional costs above that limit requiring line management sanction. Hence autonomy of front-line staff was granted within clearly defined parameters.

Closer Links with the Health Service
It was hoped to foster more effective inter-agency collaboration at the individual case level through the normal give and take of exchange relationships. Whilst budgetary decentralisation only covered the resources of one agency, this greater freedom could provide the means for a greater overall reciprocity. Thus, whenever possible, the area covered by the scheme was coterminous with that of key sectors of the health service. However, until recently, in all the areas where the scheme has operated the linkages have been on an informal basis. In one area a joint health and social care team is now working in a large group practice but this development is only as yet in its early stages.

Systematic Recording
Systematic records were developed which provided information about client characteristics, regular review of fieldworker activities and weekly costs for each case. The system was designed to provide feedback to the individual worker, accountability to management and at a more aggregated level, to provide information for strategic planning. It is described in more detail in Challis and Chesterman (1985).

Consumers, Needs and Care Practice
Increased consumer responsiveness was expected through the delivery of a more individualised approach to care. This could be seen in both the style or method of working and in the variety of needs to which effective responses were made.

Social Worker Approach and Style
It appeared that control of a budget gave fieldworkers a real incentive to undertake more careful assessments since it had become possible to devise individual and original solutions to the problems which were identified. Assessment thus became more problem-oriented, separating the identification of problems from the choice of means for their resolution. In this process, staff saw themselves as more able to involve elderly people and carers themselves closely in the definition of their needs, in identifying which areas of difficulty should be tackled, and in the choice of appropriate means to provide help. They had the resources to respond to the elderly persons' wishes about simple factors such as the time of a meal, when to retire to bed or the type of diet. The exercise of choice, maximising independence within the limits set by disability, could be a very positive experience significantly enhancing morale. The responsiveness of some elderly people to this was

marked even when previously they had been apparently very apathetic.

Mrs Z was physically frail, living in a council bungalow, frequently liable to fall and very worried about her security. She was socially isolated, had little appetite and frequently stated her indifference to living or dying though her moods tended to fluctuate. She felt that her GP and others would pay little attention to her complaints tending to ascribe them to old age. She was however determined not to enter residential care. She had been reluctant to consider help but at an early stage responded warmly to the social worker's approach which had encouraged her involvement in the identification of need and planning of care. She commented: 'All this time I have been waiting. Now you have come everything seems to be happening.' The organisation of a range of help to assist her with meal preparation, settling at night, providing companionship and assistance with her personal appearance such as hair washing, appeared to contribute to a marked improvement in her spirits. She appeared more cheerful and less anxious and later commented: 'Before you came the weekends were simply a rehearsal for death.'

In cases where families were involved in care their preferences could similarly be more realistically considered and a programme of care devised to reflect a wide range of wishes. The approach was, of course, more complicated in cases of high dependency, particularly where the elderly person suffered from mental impairment and where their capacity for recognising and defining needs was consequently limited. In such cases a more decisive approach was required, which usually involved the provision of services which appeared to suit the elderly person's needs, unless there was some evidence of explicit rejection, a procedure described by Wasser (1971) as 'protective services'. However, even the apparently simple task of finding ways of making needed help acceptable to such mentally impaired elderly people could often demand considerable ingenuity of the worker. For example, it would involve attempting to relate the help provided to retained skills so that care would be understood by the elderly person through its relationship to some retained elements of long-term memory.

Responding to a Wide Range of Needs

Much of this approach was facilitated due to closer control of resources through the decentralised budgets. Effects upon the range of responses to need were also clear. The additional budget was used in a variety of ways such as the purchase of aids and materials not usually available. However, the most frequent solution which it provided proved to be the recruitment of local people as helpers, to give assistance in a variety of ways to elderly people in addition to the contribution of established services. Where helpers were introduced to elderly people they were given a contract or letter of agreement which made explicit the tasks and objectives of care which were, wherever possible, confirmed in a three-way discussion between the social workers, the elderly person and the helper. This was designed to avoid misunderstanding and provide close involvement of the elderly person in care planning.

The continuing responsibility for cases, monitoring closely the care of elderly people, meant that frequently further needs which were not initially apparent would be uncovered and responses were demanded for these, often in ways that are not usually possible with the available range of services.

This might mean finding ways of helping people to adjust to very significant life changes. For example one man, living in a high-rise block was rendered effectively agoraphobic and experienced great difficulty in coping following the death of his wife. He was unable to accept that she had died and his rehabilitation and reinvolvement with the world only began following a programme which was arranged for him of visiting his wife's grave on a daily basis with a helper who was paid to support him.

For some individuals the existing range of services were not responsive to the ways in which their lives were restricted through disability and impairment. It was noticeable that there were a number of individuals for whom existing forms of day care were inappropriate, either because of their discomfort at a lengthy ambulance journey or for whom mental impairment was significant and thereby a day centre was experienced as bewildering and not particularly therapeutic. Localised day care, in the homes of helpers, appeared to offer for these two groups social experiences and opportunities which were beneficial and had the great advantage of continuity of attention by one or two familiar people. Interestingly, such an idea was suggested some twenty years ago by a geriatrician in London (Rosin, 1965). However, there appear to have been few reports of such an approach being developed, probably due to the organisational barriers which only decentralised budgets can readily overcome.

The needs of the elderly person's network could often be as great as the needs of the elderly person themselves. Indeed, the importance of interweaving formal and informal care has long been recognised as central to any policy of community care (Bayley, 1973). However, it is only too clear that the varied needs of carers are not always adequately met by the range of existing services. Not infrequently, existing domiciliary services can even positively discriminate against informal carers (Charlesworth *et al*, 1984). For example, it is not unknown for domiciliary help to be restricted to cleaning only that part of the house used solely by a disabled person if there is a female carer living in close proximity. It was notable that higher levels of domiciliary care were provided for those elderly people with families receiving the scheme than for comparable cases elsewhere. More importantly the help provided was fitted into the personal routines of carers recognising the great variability of their preferences. For example, where a daughter was coping with the effects of a stroke upon her father, she was helped with bathing him at a predictable time when the district nursing service found itself unable to fit into the family's preferred routine. Again, where a carer wished to go out in the evening, when facilities such as day care were unavailable, sitting-in services were developed and provided. The general focus of work for those people with informal carers was to provide support which fitted into the carers daily routine and preferences and to devise with them, realistic boundaries and limits to their involvement to prevent their being overwhelmed with the day to day drudgery of care.

The capacity of the social worker as case manager to respond more sensitively to a wide range of problems could also be seen in the responses made to problems which are frequently unmanageable within the usual range of services. One example is the *risk of falling* for elderly people living alone. Not uncommonly the fear of this event and the likely damage from the subsequent 'long lie' (Hall, 1982) may be sufficient for the elderly person to relinquish independent living, as a response both to their own anxiety and that of others. However, where their preference to remain at home was strong, it seemed that a well-coordinated plan of regular visiting was sufficient to alleviate the anxiety of the elderly person and other carers to enable them to remain at home. Even in the care of the *dementing elderly* where particularly great care problems are found, there was some degree of success in the establishment and maintenance of care and reduction of risk (Challis and Davis, 1985). Often it is difficult to establish, let alone maintain, a package of care for these people. As with other intractable problems, effective care appeared possible due to both continuing case management and the capacity to respond in a more individualised way to needs. Thus, help could be made more acceptable and 'entrée' gained to an individual's life through a variety of strategies. These included persistence, a response to particular behavioural problems, a willingness initially to provide help where need was recognised by the elderly person rather than where the need appeared greatest, and an equal concern about those elements of retained ability as a base for building care as about those areas of increasing deficit.

'Process risk', the not infrequent downward spiral of increasing self-neglect, decline and reduction of coping skills, was tackled by organising care to provide supervision, food, medication and stimulation to arrest nutritional and social decline. 'Event risk', the loss of coping skills where normal sequential acts of daily living are not completed in their entirety, such as turning on gas taps and failing to light them, causing a hazard to the elderly and their environment, was tackled by modifications to the physical environment, such as disconnecting the gas supply. Other responses to 'event risk' involved identifying regular behaviour patterns which may be repeated and establishing routines with close supervision in order to reduce the risk of wandering. Case management through 'patterning care' involved the construction of a clear and regular pattern of care based initially upon the positive elements retained by the old person despite their mental disability.

These patterns were, wherever possible, made meaningful within the old person's routine, or dependent upon external cues such as light and dark, day and night. Where there was no such routine attempts were made to create one, for example associating particular activities with retiring to bed and perhaps tiring a person at a more appropriate time, so as to provide them with a more predictable and apparently secure environment.

In one case an elderly woman appeared to have developed a pattern of wandering in the early evening which caused enormous anxiety to neighbours and family who lived not nearby since her home was not far from a river bank. It was found that she had used to gain great pleasure from knitting dishcloths and a substantial amount of dishcloth wool was purchased and every evening prior to the period when the old lady was prone to wander it was arranged for her, with a helper, to knit one or more dishcloths. It appeared as if this activity was both calming and tiring to the point where having completed the activity the old lady was usually happy to retire to bed and the restless urge seemed to have waned, being bridged by participation in constructive activity. On occasions, attention to the small and apparently insignificant details determine whether or not care was effective.

Choice about life-style could also be important. A common problem of many elderly people was poor nutrition and difficulties in meal preparation. Yet the provision of meals-on-wheels, often delivered early in the morning and providing little choice, was seen by many as a non-appetising and unsatisfactory solution. Such a service demanded little participation of the consumer either in choice or meal preparation and perhaps unsurprisingly meals were not infrequently uneaten. The need in many elderly people was not simply the provision of the meal but rather for a whole range of both practical and symbolic activities associated with meals. The provision of food alone was often insufficient to meet the care objectives of people who were mildly depressed and who tended to neglect themselves. Such people required stimulation and encouragement to eat the food whilst involvement in meal preparation with another person proved a valuable means of promoting independence. Consequently, helpers were organised to provide meals at times and of a type which suited the elderly person. Thus many objectives could be encompassed within the realm of a single activity. Even where someone had not remained in their own home as a result of the scheme the outcome could be beneficial through the extension of real choice.

Mrs V, an anxious and depressed lady, lived alone in a purpose-built bungalow for elderly people. Her main anxiety was that she was likely to fall on retiring to bed and the lack of security in the event of this occurring was coupled with debilitating loneliness. She was however concerned not to leave her own home. A support network was devised which relieved her anxiety and considerably increased her morale. However on one occasion due to illness one member of the network was unable to visit at the last minute and could not contact anyone to back her up. Mrs V found it difficult to tolerate even one incident of uncertainty and her anxiety increased again dramatically. Following a period of short-term residential care, which had fortuitously been arranged over a holiday period, it was finally decided that Mrs V should enter the home permanently. The outcome, although perhaps in some ways a failure of a scheme designed to prevent admission to residential care, was none the less acceptable, since the opportunity to stay in her own home had provided her with months of pleasure and she was able to make a realistic decision about her future in the light of wider experience of alternatives.

The Benefits and Costs of the Approach
The results from monitoring and evaluating the first pilot scheme have been described in detail elsewhere (Challis and Davies, 1984, 1985). Consequently, only a brief summary is provided here.

Effects upon Quality of Life and Quality of Care

Considerable differences were noted between those receiving the scheme over a three-year period when compared with the experience of matched cases receiving the standard range of services in an adjacent area. Over a three-year period elderly people were more likely to remain in their own homes, less likely to enter residential care and more likely to survive if they were in receipt of the scheme. This is clear from Table 9.1. Clearly, since the elderly people had expressed a preference to remain in their own homes the scheme was successful by that simple criterion.

Table 9.1:   **Location of 74 matched cases over one, two and three years receiving the community care scheme and standard services**

	Year 1		Year 2		Year 3	
	CCS	*Std Services*	CCS	*Std Services*	CCS	*Std Services*
At home	51	25	37	15	26	9
Res. care	9	20	15	25	16	23
Hospital care	3	4	2	2	6	1
Moved away	1	1	1	2	2	2
Died	10	24	19	30	24	39
	74	74	74	74	74	74

Interviews and assessments conducted with elderly people before receipt of the scheme and one year later indicated that for those in receipt of the scheme there were significant improvements in both subjective well-being, such as loneliness, and more practical indicators of quality of care, such as need for help with personal care and household care. Carers too benefited from the scheme. Felt stresses such as psychological pressure and subjective burden were significantly reduced for carers who received the scheme compared with those receiving the usual range of services. There was no significant difference between the scheme and other services in reducing practical demands upon carers, such as effects upon employment or social life. This was at first sight rather surprising, since considerable effort had been made to provide support and relief for families. It seem that, in the absence of the scheme, elderly people with carers were particularly prone to enter residential care. Entry to residential care and effective support at home likewise reduced difficulties in social life or employment. However it was clear that a carer who through lack of any other alternative had to place an elderly relative in residential care could still experience considerable guilt and distress. In such cases the scheme gave a wider range of choice not only to elderly people but also to their close informal carers.

The Costs of Care

The evidence then is that the scheme achieved its objectives in providing an opportunity for elderly people to remain in their own homes rather than enter institutional care. This appeared to have been achieved with improvements in client and carer satisfaction and quality of care. What are the resource implications of this different approach? The costs of the scheme were compared with those of providing the usual range of care to a similar group of clients. Table 9.2 shows the costs over one year for three relevant interest groups: the social services department, the National Health Service and society as a whole at 1977 prices.

Table 9.2: **Costs of care over one year (1977 prices) for matched cases receiving the community care scheme and standard services**

	Annual costs (£)		Cost per month (£)[1]	
	CCS	Std. services	CCS	Std. services
Social services department	639	702	52	59
National Health Service	778	708	69	75
Society as a Whole[2]	2850	2686	238	265

Notes:
[1]Cost per month refers to per month survived. It therefore takes account of the shorter survival period of the control group.
[2]Social opportunity costs included health and social care expenditure, the value of private housing, the old person's living expenses and directly observable financial costs borne by carers. The capital costs of hospitals, residential homes and private housing were discounted over a 60-year period at a rate of 7 per cent.

In order to allow for differences in survival patterns, costs are shown both as an annual aggregate and per month survived. The costs for the two agencies are revenue account expenditures and in the estimation of social opportunity costs a 7 per cent discount rate was applied to capital components. Due to differences in accounting procedures, the agency costs for the social services department allow for capital costs but those for the health service do not. A capital allowance was therefore estimated on the basis of an assumption of upgrading of facilities for the NHS in the social cost computations. It was not possible to include family practitioner costs in the health services estimates, but the differences between the two groups in this factor is likely to be very small. The components of social opportunity costs consisted of, therefore, the health and social care expenditures, the value of private housing and other resources consumed by the elderly person and financial costs borne by carers such as members of the family. The capital costs of hospitals, residential homes and private housing were discounted over a 60-year period at a rate of 7 per cent.

It can be seen that there is a small cost advantage to the social services department as a result of the operation of the scheme. There is little difference in costs to the National Health Service since greater longevity tended to increase costs for the community care group. However, the components of cost reveal significant differences. There was a markedly lower utilisation of residential homes and long-stay hospital beds for those elderly people receiving community care and a correspondingly greater use of domiciliary services, day hospital and acute hospital facilities. Thus, in the care of very dependent people, care in the community was clearly substituting for long-term hospital care. There were two groups of cases for whom it seemed the new approach appeared most appropriate compared with the usual range of services; that is to say, two groups for whom it was most cost effective. These were, first, the extremely dependent elderly person suffering both mental and physical frailty who receives a considerable degree of informal support. Such an observation is consistent with the conclusion of Bergmann *et al.* (1978) who indicated that to focus home care resources on the dependent elderly with informal support would be more productive, in view of the poor prognosis of those lacking informal supporters. The second group was the relatively isolated elderly person, with only a moderate degree of dependency likely to suffer from non-psychotic psychiatric disorder. These people experience difficulties which are frequently undetected in the usual range of circumstances (Kay *et al.*, 1964; Foster *et al.*, 1976).

Social Work, Consumers and Long-Term Care

The community care scheme appeared to provide an environment in which what would be described as 'good social work practice' for the elderly can develop. The new organisational arrangements provided a means of balancing the greater autonomy of front-line staff with decentralised budgets on the one hand, with their accountability to the agency and the elderly people and to provide support both directly to clients and families and indirectly to them through the support and supervision of other carers. Many of these are of course aspects of good practice but decentralisation of resources with greater autonomy provides a framework in which these aspects of good practice can cohere together. Certainly within this model, as in other settings, there is a need for staff to demonstrate competence and knowledge about a wide range of problems, available facilities and solutions if they are to appear effective to consumers (Rees and Wallace, 1982).

There are also organisational implications of such an approach. A service system which develops to provide long-term care in the community and provides personnel to perform this case management role for specific client groups will also have to provide for persons requiring less intensive and continuous interventions. In other words, for those people requiring some form of short-term care. A possible organisational structure for such a kind of system could be envisaged from a model not uncommon in many local authorities (Challis and Ferlie, 1985). This would be the division of work into a system of short-term interventions or intake teams and a series of long-term care teams organised around the needs of particular client groups. Such a model provides an opportunity, almost unique in social work, to build practice and service systems on the basis of research which has demonstrated the advantages of certain patterns of intervention both short- and long-term. This is particularly well developed in the area of short-term intervention (Reid and Shyne, 1969; Goldberg *et al.*, 1985), although a long-term care literature is emerging too (Steinberg and Carter, 1983; Challis and Davis, 1985).

We have thus far discussed a broadly professional-based solution to providing greater consumer sensitivity and involvement in care. The model of decentralised resources is built upon the norms of current effective and good practice which imply the greater influence of consumers. However, there is a danger that greater autonomy to front-line staff with larger-scale implement-ations of such a policy may require additional safeguards, or checks and balances, to ensure that clients' views continue to be a central part of the operation of the care system. A number of organisational characteristics, such as decentralised budgets with clear limits, and systematic recording have already been developed and clearly play their part in ensuring accountability. However, case management does assume that the professional takes on the role of advocate and there are obvious dangers inherent in this approach (Sang and O'Brien, 1984) where conflicts of interest can occur. The monitoring and recording procedures which ensure accountability are dependent upon information supplied by professionals and do not contain material about consumer responses. Perhaps in the longer term there will be a need for consumer surveys to become part of any management information system as has already been attempted in the NHS for hospitals (Moore and Thompson, 1985) so that further checks and balances are inserted into the care system. Professional practice too can be modified within its own norms to ensure this influence of greater plurality of interests. One such means would be the institution of regular peer-group reviews or lateral supervision to enable the dissemination of good practice between front-line staff, the sharing of information and the prevention of isolation and the ossification of approaches to care. The costs of such investment in training are clear and the costs of not doing so are perhaps in the short term not only unclear but invisible. However, if substantial changes in our approach to care, giving greater autonomy to front line workers, are contemplated it would be foolish not to consider the importance of investment in human resources for the longer term to promote quality in service provision.

Despite these caveats it is possible to see the development of case management as a clear and precise role for social work in long-term care, utilising approaches particularly well developed in the care of the mentally handicapped, such as individual patient planning, along with decentralised control of resources. An approach to care in the community which combines sensitivity and responsiveness to individual needs and wishes represents a coherent and viable way of reconciling the conflict between professional and consumerist approaches to care at the level of the individual client.

References

Bayley, M., *Mental Handicap and Community Care*, Routledge and Kegan Paul, London, 1973.

Bergmann, K., Foster, E.M., Justice, A.W. and Matthews, V., 'Management of the Demented Elderly Patient in the Community', *British Journal of Psychiatry*, 132, (1978), 441-9.

Blunden, R.,'Individual Plans for Mentally Handicapped People: A draft procedural guide', Mental Handicap in Wales, Applied Research Unit, Cardiff, 1980.

Challis, D. and Chesterman, J., 'A System for Monitoring Social Work Activity with the Frail Elderly', *British Journal of Social Work*, 15, (1985), 115-32.

Challis, D. and Davies, B., 'Community Care Schemes: a development in the home care of the frail elderly', in Evans, J. Grimley and Caird, F.I. (eds), *Advanced Geriatric Medicine 4*, Pitman, London, 1984.

Challis, D. and Davies, B., 'Long-term Care for the Elderly: The Community Care Scheme', *British Journal of Social Work*, 15 (1985), 563-79.

Challis, D. and Ferlie, E.,'Reorganisation: All Change - But Which Way?,' *Community Care*, Feb. 13, 1986, 19-21.

Charlesworth, A., Wilkin, D. and Durie, A., *Carers and Services: A comparison of men and women caring for dependent elderly people*, Equal Opportunities Commission, London, 1984.

Foster, E.M., Kay, D.W.K. and Bergmann, K.,'The Characteristics of Old People Receiving and Needing Domiciliary Services: The Relevance of Diagnosis', *Age and Ageing*, 5 (1976), 245-55.

Frankfather, D.L., Smith, M.J. and Caro, F.G., *Family Care of the Elderly*, Heath, Lexington, Mass., 1981.

Glendenning, C.,'The Resource Worker Project: Evaluating a Specialist Social Work Service for Severely Disabled Children and their Families', *British Journal of Social Work*, 14 (1984), 103-16.

Goldberg, E.M. and Connelly, N., *The Effectiveness of Social Care for the Elderly*, Heinemann, London, 1982.

Goldberg, E.M. and Warburton, R.W., *Ends and Means in Social Work*, Allen and Unwin, London, 1979.

Goldberg, E.M., Gibbons, J. and Sinclair, I., *Problems, Tasks and Outcomes: The evaluation of task-centred casework in three settings*, Allen and Unwin, London, 1985.

Sang, R. and O'Brien, J., *Advocacy*, Kings Fund Centre, London, 1984.

Steinberg, R.M. and Carter, G.W., *Case-Management and the Elderly*, Heath, Lexington, Mass., 1983.

Stevenson, O., and Parsloe, P., *Social Services Teams: The practitioners view*, HMSO, London, 1978.

Wade, B., Sawyer, L. and Bell, J., *Dependency with Dignity*, Bell, London, 1984.

Wasser, E., 'Protective Practice in Serving the Mentally Impaired Aged', *Social Casework*, 52 (1971), 510-2.

Wolfenberger, W., 'The Definition of Normalisation: Update, problems, disagreements and misunderstandings, in Flynn, R.J. and Nitsch, K. (eds), *Normalisation, Social Integration and Community Services*, University Park Press, Baltimore, 1980.

10 Consumers in Mental Health Planning: 'The Camden Consortium'
Christopher Heginbotham

Background

A lot has been said and written recently about consumer involvement in planning and development of mental health services, yet few working examples exist as lessons for future activity. This chapter describes one approach to involving local people, consumers of mental health services and interested professionals in discussing and developing ideas for improved local mental health services. The case study describes the development of what has become known as the 'Camden Consortium' – a loose grouping of consumers, professionals and local people involved one way or another in the delivery of mental health care.

Planning of mental health services has often been bureaucratic, health service-dominated and imbued with the medical model of care to the exclusion of other approaches to support and help for mentally ill people. The Camden Consortium was one attempt to break out of the rigid planning framework and develop a new way forward.

Beginnings

Camden is both an exciting and frustrating borough in which to have active involvement. On the one hand the Labour-controlled local authority has been farsighted during the last fifteen years in developing alternative strategies for mental health and mental handicap care. Whilst subject to grant penalty and ratecapping, Camden social services committee currently spends over £32 million per annum on its social services for a population of some 180,000 people. Although the mental health services run by the borough can hardly be described as a comprehensive network, Camden provides more mental health facilities per head of population than almost any other area of the country. Even so, huge gaps still exist. But in comparison to an area like Kent, for example, Camden spends four times as much per annum per capita on social services; or to take another example, Camden has more mental health facilities run by the borough (or funded by the borough through voluntary agencies) than a city like Glasgow.

On the other hand, Camden is frustratingly split into two health authorities.

Hampstead District Health Authority runs the Royal Free teaching hospital, a huge monolithic 830-bed unit requiring very substantial resources. As well as being a district general hospital it contains regional specialities in liver transplantation, virology, neuro-surgery, haemophilia, renal dialysis, and many more. In the south of the borough the University College Hospital is also a major consumer of health care resources, both money and staff, and again provides other regional specialities, including ear, nose and throat, and tropical diseases. At the same time the Bloomsbury District Health Authority cuts across two boroughs – in other words it is not coterminus with either local authority – Camden or Westminster – and was set up ostensibly to merge the Middlesex teaching hospital and University College Hospital. It is one of the biggest districts in the country with a budget of well over £100 million.

All of this background is relevant because much of the energy of administrators and health authority members is diverted into the acute specialities and the running of these major hospitals. Camden is atypical in other ways, being an Inner London borough with three major railway stations – Euston, St Pancras and Kings Cross – within its boundaries, and the health authorities also run other national units. Hampstead District Health Authority for example contains within its boundaries the Tavistock Institute and manages ex-territorially Coppetts Wood Isolation Hospital. One very clear irony in Camden is the large sums spent on mental health services which provide only a tiny service to the borough.

So Camden is not typical and yet contains all the ingredients for creating additional complexities in the planning process. Friern Hospital serves four districts – Hampstead, Bloomsbury, Islington and Haringey. Though managed by Hampstead District Health Authority, Friern clearly looks to those other boroughs and district health authorities both in the provision of its services and in consideration of its own future management – if and when it is decentralised and split up between those districts.

Discussions about the future of Friern Hospital have been going on as long as anyone can remember. In the mid-1960s the report 'Sans Everything' on the paucity of care in Friern Hospital made a number of politicians sit up and take note. Following the Ely and Farley enquiries Richard Crossman appointed Peggy Jay as Chair of the Hospital Management Committee under the old North East Regional Hospital Board charged with improving conditions in the hospital and reducing the numbers of patients. Over the last 25 years the in-patient population at Friern has fallen from some 2000 to around 820 today. At the same time the budget in real terms has continued to increase and Friern now consumes some £12 million per annum to pay for 30 psychiatrists, 670 nurses and around 450 ancilliary staff of one sort or another. The cost per annum per capita is higher than average at around £14,000 per annum as against £12,090 per annum generally within England and Wales (1983–84 figures). The site at Friern is probably one of the most valuable in the country with 65 acres just off the North Circular in Barnet.

Following the 1973/74 Health Service reorganisation and the setting-up of

Community Health Councils, the first task of the North Camden CHC was to look at mental health and mental handicap services. A report issued by the CHC in 1977 was deeply critical of the lack of development of alternative services to Friern and the need for urgent action to find ways of developing a community health service with the attendant rundown of the large hospital. Not surprisingly, there was considerable reaction from staff within the hospital. Eventually Dr Jim Glancy was asked to prepare a report on Friern and on the potential for development of alternatives. This report was inconclusive and was followed by a three-member Commission from the then Camden and Islington Area Health Authority who also looked into the possibilities for change. They reported that alternatives should be provided before the hospital could be run down but pointed to the need for substantial additional capital investment and additional revenue money to fund the transition.

By 1982 the Health Service had been reorganised yet again and Camden and Islington were split into the three District Health Authorities – Islington, Hampstead and Bloomsbury. At this time Paul Walker, the Regional Medical Officer in the North East Thames Regional Health Authority and someone who for a long time had been interested in the ways in which alternative mental health services could be provided, put some energy into promoting change. The Regional Health Authority agreed that they would seek a strategy from the District Health Authorities in the catchment of Friern and Claybury Hospitals for developing alternatives to those hospitals with the aim of closure over a maximum 10-year period. Unfortunately, just before this was to be announced to staff, the Regional Medical Officer appeared on the television and the first that staff heard of it was that TV report. Many staff have still not forgotten what they consider to have been an insult.

None the less the District Health Authorities then set about developing what they called 'User' reports on the basis that they were 'consumers' of services from Friern; and Friern itself with the Region prepared a 'Provider' report. Hampstead was put in a curious position of being both provider and user. None the less the five reports went forward to the Region. Although the 'Provider' report was critical of the possibilities of developing alternatives, and the 'User' reports were positive but required considerable additional finance, the Region in July 1983 took the decision that they wished to start planning in detail for alternative service provision and the closure or rundown of Friern Hospital. The Regional Health Authority then set a tight time-scale for Districts to plan in some detail the sort of services they would like to see. At first they suggested approximately a nine-month time-scale from July 1983 which proved totally impossible. But this was the catalyst for setting up the 'Camden Consortium'.

During the 'User' group discussions no 'real consumers' had been involved and few representatives of the community or local voluntary agencies. The tight time-scale suggested by the Region encouraged a number of local people, including members of the Health Authority who were unhappy at the planning process, ex-patients of Friern, staff of community and hospital mental health services and CHC members to feel that now was the time to set up a participative mechanism both as an end in itself and as a way of promoting new ideas to the Health Authority and the Local Authority. The aim at this time was not to get involved in the time-consuming business of commenting on District or Regional plans but to try to put positive alternative proposals for debate.

Camden Consortium: A Start

Getting started proved rather difficult. A core group consisting of a member of the Health Authority (the author), a journalist who happened to be a member of the CHC, the Mental Health Service Development Officer of Camden Local Authority and the Secretary of Hampstead CHC called a meeting of a fairly small group of interested people. This included the Chair of the Local Association for Mental Health, social workers and nursing staff and one or two other local people. With the Region's time-scale in mind, the group agreed it would be necessary to get together some sort of alternative view quite quickly. A working party was established which was intended to meet just before Christmas 1983 to put together some sort of statement and which could then be placed before the Health Authority. Unfortunately, because of the tight time-scale and because of the time of year, the group was unable to meet and by the end of January the process had got no further. With hindsight it is clear that the energy for this particular approach had really not been communicated to all members of the group and there was still uncertainty and lack of cohesion about the best approach. During the early part of 1984 it became obvious that none of the Health Authorities would meet the Region's deadline, and the Regional Health Authority would have to delay to some degree.

Consequently the core group met again and felt that the total membership should be widened to try to involve as many people as possible in an alternative form of debate. Invitations were then sent out widely to medical and para-medical staff in Friern and the Royal Free Psychiatric Unit, to social work and social services staff, to voluntary agencies and to local people and consumers seeking their involvement in a joint meeting to consider the future of mental health care. This meeting took place at the Camden Association for Mental Health Day Centre in Kentish Town and was well attended.

Membership of the group was extremely broad. Meeting at the Camden Association Drop-In Centre in an evening meant that a number of ex-patients of Friern Hospital were able to be present. In addition two psychiatrists from the hospital came to the meetings, social work staff from the hospital attended and so did two CPNs, residential care workers and a number of other local interested people. After early discussion about what the Consortium should or could try to achieve, some sort of administration seemed to be needed to keep the process moving. No one wished to become Convenor of the group at this stage which was no bad thing but did lead to confusion with others who wanted to get involved. This was particularly the case for psychiatrists who found difficulty communicating with the group as a whole and needed to discuss matters with a Chair or Convenor. The constant factor throughout, however, was the invaluable support of Hampstead Community Health Council, in particular its then Secretary, who continued to provide administrative back-up, sending out invitations, photocopying and generally providing support. Without that help the Consortium would have folded very quickly.

During the early summer of 1984 the Consortium met about monthly in attempts to define what sort of service might be appropriate. Some focus was needed but was difficult to achieve. After lengthy and searching discussion it was agreed to produce the first of what was hoped to be a series of booklets looking at the sort of mental health service the Consortium would like to see. Don Braisby, the Camden Mental Health Development Officer, and the author were charged with trying to produce some sort of statement about services for adults with long-term disabilities. A first draft was produced and presented to the Consortium. Interestingly, at the meeting at which the draft was discussed, one of the psychiatrists from Friern tried to open up the whole debate again, rather than consider the more narrow compass of the report. This would have undermined the process of having a focus on a particular subject and led to considerable disagreement between that person and others within the group. At this point the lack of a specific person chairing or convening the group did cause some difficulties. Interestingly, the group overcame this quite well.

After some debate as to the substance of the paper it was given general agreement by the Consortium – though not by everyone by any means. As a way of getting the ideas over to the planners and the public alike the Consortium felt that the paper ought to be printed and MIND was able to provide a small grant towards the cost. Consequently by the end of August 1984, the Consortium issued its first paper, 'Towards a Local Comprehensive Mental Health Service – No. 1 Services for Adults with Long-Term Disabilities'. The paper was largely written by Don Braisby with input from Consortium members and set out the principles of the sort of services that the Consortium would like to see, based strongly on the balanced service system approach. This approach seeks to understand the needs that individuals have in terms of matching functions of a mental health service rather than the traditional concepts of day care, housing, day hospitals, etc. From this, the document looked at a model of local mental health care which could be developed and how this might relate to existing and planning services within the borough.

The 'Disruptor'

Whilst it can hardly be said that the paper was well received it did get read, mainly because of the next and what proved to be the most crucial event in the Consortium's development. Consortium agreed to hold a study day at the

King's Fund Centre, fortunately situated in Camden, and to invite representatives of psychiatry, nursing, para-medical staff, the local community and patients or ex-patients and carers. Members of the Health Authority and administration were also invited and at the final count some 60 people were there on the day. Quite a number of people read the document who would not otherwise have done so and were pushed into discussing more fully the issues involved.

Fortuitously the date chosen for the workshop coincided with a visit of the Health Advisory Service to Friern Hospital, and a member of the HAS Team attended the workshop. To what extent this was important in the long run can only be conjecture. It meant however that there were representatives of almost every faction involved in the debate about the future of the hospital. The day consisted of presentations by staff at Friern Hospital, at the Royal Free Psychiatric Unit, social services day and residential facilities, of community nursing and the voluntary sector. Although it was obvious during the debate that there was still very substantial disagreement as to how far services could be localised and the extent to which consumers, carers and local people could be involved, looking back it is now obvious that the day had a substantial effect on the thinking of a number of key people involved in the planning process.

The District Planning Team of Hampstead Health Authority was still tackling disagreements over how a service could be provided. Up to September 1984 the model it had developed was still heavily rooted in a medical approach and based on large medical units within the community. Although the proposed alternatives to Friern were situated in Camden, by no stretch of the imagination could the plan be considered a localised, or in any way 'normalised', mental health service. Following the King's Fund workshop, medical, para-medical and lay members of the Health Authority and the Planning Team rethought a number of their ideas. Whilst the final District Planning Team report to the Health Authority could hardly be called a model for a truly localised comprehensive mental health service it does now incorporate two core and cluster schemes, fewer beds in the centralised medical units and a greater openness towards developing local staff teams.

Indeed, the proposed service, although more expensive than the Region will presently allow, would certainly be a better service than that currently provided at Friern Hospital. So if nothing else, there is now a plan which could be put into operation, which is probably acceptable to most people as far as it goes, and which could be changed and modified over a period of time towards a more local, flexible and democratic service.

Perhaps more importantly though the day at the King's Fund proved to be catalytic to the Camden Consortium. It was possible to encourage others to come along as it could be seen that the Consortium was doing something. Holding a day conference of that sort encouraged representatives of other groups that had not been involved – for example, a number of representatives of Camden Committee for Community Relations attended. They were rightly critical of the lack of black and minority ethnic representatives on the

Consortium. This criticism was accepted and the invitation list widened as an attempt to involve others from all the communities in Camden. The workshop day was also an impetus to the Consortium doing more work. Following that day the Consortium felt it should tackle other aspects of services, to look perhaps at the needs of children, those of adolescents, acute adult illness services, the needs of elderly mentally infirm people, the mental health issues concerned with black and minority ethnic communities, and the mental health of women.

At the next meeting after the workshop day attendance was much higher with more consumers present. A number of working groups were established within the Consortium by consumers to consider various issues. Many were particularly critical of some of the current provision made for them. Setting up the groups was a useful exercise in itself as it encouraged those who were shy or unused to being involved in a large group – the Consortium had become a group of 30 to 40 people – to be able to contribute to the debate.

At around this time in mid-autumn 1984, meetings were held at an alternative venue, a Camden Social Service Day Centre. Although this Centre was only half a mile from the Camden Association for Mental Health Drop-In Centre, the effect over a period of three months or so was for the consumer members of the Consortium to change. For the next meeting one or two of the consumers, who felt their base to be the Camden Association Centre came to the new venue, but by the beginning of 1985 the balance of consumers involved were those who attend the Day Centre and not the Camden Association Centre. Thus some of the particularly articulate and important members of the Consortium who had been involved in the earlier stages were temporarily lost to the debate and others became involved. On the one hand, it is clearly a good thing to have change and development, yet here it was perhaps occurring for the wrong reasons. Some of the earlier participants wished to continue involvement but may have felt excluded at the new venue.

A tendency developed amongst some professional staff to manipulate, in the most low-key way and often for the best of motives, the ways in which the consumers were considering the issues. Where a staff role is concerned with growth and therapy rather than voluntary counselling or social involvement this may explain the tendency among some of those involved to 'see behind' what the consumers were saying. A tendency to interpret rather than record faithfully is one which must be resisted as far as possible.

A Tendency to Interpret?

Setting up local participative structures is not easy, especially if the subject is complex. For example, the development of tenant accountability and area committees of Housing Departments and Housing Associations has often been slow for two principle reasons – lack of information and lack of consumer power.

People who have traditionally been denied any sort of power or control need help, sometimes cajoling, certainly moral and practical support, to come to grips with difficult issues – for example, the complicated form of accounts of Housing Associations. It is not that those tenants or consumers are inherently any less able to understand the issues, but quite simply that access to the information in a reasonably assimilable form has been denied. Staff need to provide teaching sessions, seminars and materials at times and in places convenient to the consumers and users of services. This may mean teaching on a ward, or spending time writing out complex issues in jargon-free language.

In local participative fora information is power. Consumers or tenants cannot take decisions without proper information. They must also be given help in the most non-threatening, least paternalistic way to articulate their ideas. This may be especially necessary for those on heavy drug dosages, or people with long-term disabilities as a result of illness. Many consumers may be fearful of ridicule or embarrassment in speaking on subjects in front of professional staff; and for some there is the ever-present fear of the next-day power of the professional once outside the more cosy confines of the participative group.

None of this is new! But so often professionals whilst paying lip-service to sympathetic considerations of these points fail to work hard enough to ensure that as many barriers to open informed discussion are broken down or lowered.

Fresh Energy

By the beginning of 1985 the Consortium was somewhat in the doldrums. A new impetus was needed and fresh energy required to generate involvement and a feeling of belonging to a group which was achieving something. The answer was unclear yet gradually fresh energy emerged as the consumers themselves with help from a few very good and committed professionals gradually took a greater share in the administration and development of the Consortium.

One aspect indicated by this is the cyclical nature of such groups. If there is insufficient time or energy amongst a number of people who are particularly interested then other energy may flag. It also illustrates one of the substantial contradictions which has to be overcome. To get off the ground a Consortium of this sort does need a core group of people who are committed to the aims of participation, who have some understanding of the issues and access to resources, but who do not wish to dominate the future of the group. As with any sharing or participative group, especially where the potential members of the group have for many years been denied access to decision making processes, there is a tendency for one or two people to dominate. Or, if those individuals do take a back seat or try to slip away, the energy may be removed. Shifting the energy for change onto other members of the group and ensuring continuity requires deft timing if early participants wish to move on to something else. And in any event this all smacks of a rather paternalistic approach though one which has to be recognised as a necessary preliminary to the development of a forum such as the Consortium with a role and a shared commitment to continue the debate. As long as professional staff recognise the nature of the paternalism and are truly committed to sharing information, and sharing or devolving power, that early stage can be overcome. Many consumers however have themselves said that they welcome the guidance of professionals in putting ideas together, suggesting alternatives and finding ways of promoting the ideas that emerge.

Objectives

As the sub-groups worked on, and the group held together, the minutes began to make both exciting and informative reading. Some members had been unable to attend many meetings (including the author) but a strong central group remained. By spring 1985 Terms of Reference for the group had been drawn up in connection with the Constitution. These terms, or objectives, eventually were stated as:

1. To bring together a wide range of people who have a shared interest in mental health in Camden, in particular people with direct experience of mental health services and relatives and friends of service users;
2. to provide a forum for the discussion of mental health services and issues;
3. to promote a coherent consumer view in relation to mental health in Camden;
4. to highlight unmet needs, campaign for necessary resources and initiate or sponsor improved services.

One of the working groups then produced a useful paper, 'Consumer Views – Mental Health Priorities for Planners'. From this came a very strong articulation on the need for psychiatric services to treat people as human beings. The Consortium identified the admission process to hospital as crucial and current hospital procedures as heightening the feeling of 'losing control'. A 'lack of individual attention' was noted, and a tendency to devalue the person at a time of crisis – a sort of psychiatric 'Catch 22'.

At the same time that the working group was meeting, members had discussed the need for another conference, both to launch the Consortium formally, to enhance cohesion of the group and to continue public debate on the issues. The subject of psychiatric 'Catch 22' was the obvious choice and the event should take place in early 1986.

Lessons

In conclusion it is probably worth drawing out some of the lessons of the Camden experience. There have of course been mistakes, but more importantly there have been lessons which perhaps could not easily have been foreseen and which may be helpful to others. On a trivial level it is difficult to set up a new organisation just before Christmas or a major holiday period. Timing for the flotation of such a venture is crucial. More significantly, there is a need to ensure a shared commitment and vision amongst the first group of participants. If early catalysers of the group leave too quickly without passing on the energy the group may fail quite quickly. At the same time a commitment to sharing and mutual support is also vital.

Secondly, there is a serious danger in a group of this sort that it simply chases its tail, discussing meeting after meeting the same issues and going round and round in circles. Some form of direction or leadership is needed even if that is of a very low-key kind. If such direction can come from a group of people sharing the tasks of convening and involving others so much the better. Perhaps a good model would be a collective executive core of six or seven people who can share the major tasks associated with running the group. Good committed professional staff with the right skills can facilitate such a group as long as they remain aware of the servicing role and the need to share and rotate tasks and to support those previously denied involvement to take on responsibility.

Thirdly, involving medical and para-medical staff is important and worthwhile. Although it may lead to deeper divisions and splits within the group and a more polarised debate, at the end of the day it can be no bad thing for community activists to know what psychiatrists are thinking, and for psychiatrists to have an understanding of the very different position taken by a group, such as the consumer representatives in the Consortium.

Fourthly, the CHC was an extremely helpful source of administrative resources without which the Consortium would not have got going. Administrative help is essential, and so is small amounts of money for telephone, stamps and so on. And fifthly, tapping into resources such as the King's Fund Centre obviously helped enormously.

A sixth lesson is the value of producing some sort of publication for debate. A loose grouping of local people, volunteers and professional staff needs a focus and some reason for coherent action. A publication can be that focus and can help the debate along as occurred in Camden. That publication used as a 'disruptor' can have substantial effect, as many community groups will testify. In the Camden case the first paper on adults with long-term disabilities was important in making a number of members of the District Planning Team think again or read publications offering an alternative vision. The paper put up an alternative horizon which should be considered. Of course the paper, the meeting and subsequent events have not changed the minds of all involved. But it threw a spanner in the works at a key moment – an important tactic which must not be lost in the future.

Finally a lesson which must be learnt is that people with long-term mental illnesses or disabilities resulting from mental illness need time and help in the least patronising way to be involved in such a process. Shifting the venue from one centre to another will not always be helpful to a number of participants; though of course developing small groups based on each of the centres, then coming together in some collective sense, perhaps on a borough-wide basis, may well be a useful approach to take. But there is a tendency for staff, however hard they try, to feel that they can interpret what consumers or patients are trying to say, especially if what the consumers are saying is threatening to the staff's particular jobs or way of life. Offering consumers (of any service) a real voice means that they are likely to disagree with the staff of that service.

One of the substantial challenges of the next ten years in mental health service development is to design models of care which are flexible not only in terms of finance but in how staff can adapt to the changing needs of the consumers and the changing ethos of care. Local participative managements, decentralised and devolved decision-making, are all important, though staff require, and must be given, supervision, support, training and guidance. Working at the sharp end is difficult and staff burnout will continue to occur without proper supportive systems. Yet the whole tenor of the approach of the Consortium and what it implies is that services should be geared to the needs of the individual rather than geared to the staffing patterns, current buildings or bureaucracy.

Conclusion

The Camden Consortium has taught a number of us a lot of lessons. It has been an interesting development, and one which will undoubtedly continue. It is not a consumer-only group and this makes it different from those groups which do not involve anyone other than those who have experienced mental health services at first hand. It may not be the model for every area, but is one approach to developing a local forum, obtaining greater participation of local people, local communities, consumers and professional staff; and demonstrates that if we are serious about consumer involvement and participation it can be done even if it has some difficulties.

The final lesson is a very positive one. In the long term, developments such as the Camden Consortium can only improve the mental health care in the community and help us to generate localised supportive networks staffed by appropriately trained personnel and with the attendant closure of the large institutions.

11 Self-Help and Consumerism: 'The Experience of the Nottingham Self-Help Team' *Judy Wilson*

'If we get together and shout loud enough, they've got to listen to us.' A desperate parent whose child was a glue-sniffer had met with other parents for the first time. She was bewildered by her son's actions, isolated from much of her community because of it, and despairing about getting help from any of the statutory services. Though a new group, they had plenty of ideas of what they could do, and drawing attention to the lack of care and resources from professional workers came high on their list. But was it necessarily true that they would be listened to? Do self-help groups campaign effectively? And, indeed, do they want to? With the big growth of self-help groups in recent years, it is worth examining this and other aspects of consumerism as it relates to mutual aid groups.

But generalising about self-help groups is very difficult. With this proviso, let us look at three particular aspects of consumerism: first, the extent to which they offer services, and so a choice for the person in need; secondly, how much they feed back comment on services and resources to policy-makers, and service providers – and to what extent, they want to do this, or are allowed to; and thirdly, whether there is any relationship between self-help groups and consumer involvement in personal problem-solving.

We need however to consider both the extent to which groups generally wish to undertake any activity beyond the mutual support which is at the core of the work of most of them, and how far professionals let them contribute in any way. Does professional and political encouragement of self-help groups, or a particular aspect of their work, in fact lead to direct or indirect control? This is an aspect of self-help groups developed elsewhere after a visit to West Berlin (Wilson, 1985). People form and join self-help groups to meet their own needs. One cannot assume that there is a particular pattern or trend, or any wish to see their activity as a logical part of the pattern of social services.

The Work of Self-Help Groups
What are self-help groups? How widespread are they? What do they do? Let us first briefly look at these questions. Ann Richardson and Meg Goodman whose perceptive account of four self-help organisations and their local

branches is one of the few pieces of careful research published in this country (Richardson and Goodman, 1983), defines them as 'groups of people who feel they have a common problem (typically concerning a medical, social or behavioural condition) and have joned together to try to do something about it'.

Little is known about their numbers or coverage, the only brief survey being carried out as long ago as 1979 (Levy, 1982). It seems clear however that they are growing both in numbers and in the range of conditions on which they are based. People must find them helpful, otherwise they would not continue.

It is not easy, as has been said, to generalise about their activities. A majority, probably concentrate on mutual support and a great many aim to provide information. Others, who may merge into the category of voluntary organisations, provide services and some concentrate on fundraising, often for national organisations or for research. Self-help groups vary, as we shall see, in their interest in campaigning. Lastly, a common thread among their activities is the opportunity they give to people who are over the worst of their problem to be useful – members' motives vary for attending, but some probably go for this alone, and many come to find satisfaction in this role. They are not a coherent, easily understandable set of groups. Many are vulnerable, inconsistent and some are short-lived. They have immense strengths and achieve a great deal, but cannot be approached as if they were a predictable set of organisations, as one might Marriage Guidance Councils or Citizen's Advice Bureaux.

As two of the editors of this book have said, consumers of welfare services are often in a particularly vulnerable position, both socially and emotionally (Etherington and Parker, 1985). Those who join groups are not immune to this, and the groups themselves are often handicapped by the effects of the particular condition on which they are based. Other common problems facing groups are lack of experience of organising, over-ambition as to what they can achieve, lack of resources, hostility or inertia among professionals, lack of visibility and domination by a few key members. While some belong to a national umbrella organisation, a majority either do not at all or get very little support from it.

Local Support

It was with these constraints in mind that Nottingham Self-Help Groups Project (now the Self-Help Team) was set up in 1982. A detailed account of its early work has been published elsewhere (Wilson, 1983) and a further study is in preparation (Unell, forthcoming). Its work was based on the need for support – but giving groups the option to take it up – and the untapped potential there is in our community for more self-help groups, or increased activity by existing ones. These two concepts – the need for support and latent potential – are two further key ideas in this examination of self-help groups as consumers.

Three areas of work by the Self-Help Team have proved to be particularly useful, in what is now seen to be a generally successful piece of work. These are: information and publicity about self-help groups; individual support to new groups; and local networking between a cross-section of very different local self-help groups. The last three years has seen a big increase in the number of groups in Nottingham, and some of this can be contributed to the existence of the Team. There has been too increased visibility of groups; a more general appreciation for groups to learn and grow. A local resource and information centre for self-help groups is not the only way support can be given, but its existence has demonstrated the value of having identifiable back-up services, and the way in which lay potential can be released. Not all groups need or want our services, and there must be no thought of coercing groups into any particular structure. The heavy use though, made of our services, has confirmed the hunch on which the scheme was originally based.

A Self-Help Movement?

Bearing in mind this need for support and the vulnerability and lack of experience of many groups, let us return to self-help groups' involvement and interest in consumerism. There is no doubt that they are part of a wider movement of people concerned to participate and be involved in their community. It is questionable whether there is a self-help movement as such, but it can be seen as part of a general interest and concern among ordinary people to be involved. Self-help group members often want to be in charge of part of their lives, to enjoy being part of a relatively small group. They identify with other people who are finding tension in their relationship with professionals and tend to form relatively informal and sometimes temporary groups. In these and other ways, they share much with other kinds of development in other consumer-centred organisations or campaigning groups, and it is appropriate to consider their particular contribution to consumerism.

Three specific aspects were outlined at the beginning of this chapter, the first being the provision of services by self-help groups, and the extent to which they can be seen as offering choice to the consumer.

Self-Help Groups as Service Providers

Let's look at three different local groups. How far are they able to offer services to their members, or to the public at large? 'Friends in Need' is a small neighbourhood-based group of parents of handicapped children. Their weekly meeting is at the core of their activities, and despite problems of premises, transport and lack of care for the children, they have continued to meet for three years. They've had speakers, gone on outings and run social and fund-raising events. But they cannot be seen as offering a comprehensive range of services, and only the members who have been coming for some time they say, gain great advantage from the group.

A branch of the 'Alzheimer's Disease Society' dwindled to three members, two of them currently caring for parents with senile dementia. Without local and national support and encouragement, the group could well have closed down. Now, with more resources, including back-up from a social worker, it is thriving and about to open a day centre one day a week. Their concern is that there are so few resources available for people in this situation, and in the current financial climate, it is unlikely that enough will be provided. The motivation for providing a service is desperation, and despair that professional care will ever meet their needs.

'Anorexic Aid' often gets requests from despairing people too. Some of their members continue to receive psychiatric help while also attending meetings, but many people come to the group as an alternative. But the fortnightly meetings of this small group can hardly be said to be a formal service, and the group deliberately does not publicise telephone numbers. They are mostly still vulnerable themselves and are clear they cannot operate as an alternative emergency service.

Constraints on the Provision of Services

It is difficult to say to what extent these groups are typical of others round the country. They do illustrate however the constraints on services than can be provided by groups, and the deliberate policy adopted by some of not being a service provider. For there can be real disadvantages – 'AA' (Alcoholics Anonymous) has recognised this in one of its twelve traditions, conscious that outside enterprises can lead to a situation where 'problems of money, property and prestige divert us from our primary purpose'. Preoccupation with services may prevent a group from offering effective mutual support, and lose the freshness and flexibility that is often their hallmark. And providing services themselves could be said to give statutory services the excuse not to include what is needed in their own pattern of care. Some, perhaps more politically aware groups, realise this and prefer to campaign for better state services rather than run their own.

Lastly, even if groups are offering some services – and it is doubtful if this happens to any large extent – can there be said to be choice if people in need do not know about them? Publicity about self-help groups is not adequate and people in need do not always get to know that they exist, let alone provide a service.

One must conclude that there are definite limits on the interest or capacity of self-help groups to provide services. While some will want to, it is probably more helpful to see their contribution as largely complementary to professional care, rather than as a total alternative. There are exceptions of course, and current economic trends may force people to provide their own care. But it would be wrong to base a policy of care on a premise that self-help groups are a vehicle for substantial services.

Self-Help Groups as Commentators

Individual consumers of health and welfare services find it very difficult to comment on the care they have received, or on the amount that is available. They do not wish to create more problems for themselves, find feedback daunting and sometimes impossible, do not wish to appear to criticise helpful individuals and are afraid of prejudicing the possibility of future care for themselves and their dependants.

But they are sources of valuable information. Providers of social services should be finding out what consumers think: comment through self-help groups are one way of getting over the problems that individual consumers undoubtedly have. Groups based on specific conditions avoid too some of the problems associated with patch-based groups: concern has been voiced (Clode, Etherington and Parker, this volume) that vocal, middle-class areas will, by being more organised and confident, attract more resources for their neighbourhood and so themselves. Groups relating to a particular problem rather than a geographical area will be likely to be representative of a wider cross-section of people. Research has shown that they often cover a range of classes (Richardson and Goodman) and any success in their campaigns are likely to result in resources being available for anyone with the same condition, not just the better-off.

Groups are often in a strong position, sometimes stronger than they realise. There is often great public sympathy for their problems; they can speak about them from first-hand experience; and they have little to lose by speaking out. Commenting on services publicly can often help too to destigmatise conditions. A final benefit for members is that they often feel so much better if they are at least trying to do something constructive.

But some groups – and 'AA' is again an example – deliberately choose not to campaign or comment. In enthusiasm for the potential of self-help groups in this field, one must not imply that they should undertake it. Members themselves decide on their activities and priorities, and must not be forced into taking on such a role.

Achievements and Constraints

Where groups do choose this task, what achievements have there been? And, more importantly in this context, what are the constraints on their ability to campaign effectively?

Two examples of local groups show what can be done. A local branch of the 'Partially Sighted Society' became concerned about low branches of trees overhanging pavements but didn't know quite how to go about tackling the problem. They had the opportunity to raise this informally with the chairman of the County Council at a reception put on for self-help groups. He contacted the relevant department, the local paper publicised the case and the public at large were alerted to the dangers.

A branch of the 'Diabetic Association' had close links with local medical and other professional workers. A panel discussion technically arranged for patients to ask questions, gave the opportunity for feedback on organisation of clinics and how new patients felt. The doctors began to ask the questions and to listen to the answers.

Two elements are both present here: access and interaction. Both would seem essential for easy comment and feedback. For it is not an easy business, and there are considerable constraints on the opportunities and potential effectiveness of self-help groups wanting to work in this way. Let us consider four in particular:

1. General difficulties surrounding many self-help groups, already touched on. A group needs a strong base before it can take on a dialogue with those in control.
2. Lack of knowledge of how systems operate. The operation of health and social services is complex enough for professionals and politicians: it can prove to be a real barrier for self-help group members.
3. Emphasis on campaigning may inhibit other work of self-help groups, in the same way as the provision of services may do. Feedback and evolving ideas are time-consuming and lengthy. People may prefer to use their limited energy and time – they are after all acting as volunteers – in mutual support for each other.
4. Structured ways of involving consumers may be too formal for self-help groups. And yet, professionals are often reluctant to evolve informal ways of communicating, or to give time to listening.

In conclusion, there is immense potential here for increasing the opportunities for self-help groups, to contribute in this way. Many of them would respond more, in my view, if they could operate from a generally stronger base, and were offered a range of opportunities rather than one formal way of interaction. The formation of alliances between groups might well strengthen their case and increase their resources.

Self-Help Groups and Individual Care
Discussion at self-help group meetings can often revolve around the way in which individuals have been treated by professionals. Their often justified complaints tend to concentrate not so much on treatment and services, but on the attitude of the professional worker to the individual client or patient. The very terminology is uncomfortable, implying that the professional knows best. And of course, very often they do. But what many individuals want, and respond to, is a chance to be a partner in plans for the diagnosis and treatment of their problem. This applies not only to the person with the problem but to close relatives who may be very involved in their care. Families are often particularly despairing about the lack of consultation and involvement. There appears to be change here, in social work at least, but there is still far to go.

The Development of Self-Confidence
Where do self-help groups fit in? Their importance, I feel, is as much in the way they help people grow in confidence and skills, as in the way they help them cope with their actual condition. What could be called the 'self-help process', that comes from involvement in a successful self-help group, allows an individual to have more self-confidence and grow in personal development.

With this comes a confidence of their ability to share care with professionals and be more assertive about the need for partnership and involvement. Many self-help groups will in fact encourage members to approach their individual problems in this way. Finding that other people have experienced the same may be enough for other members. Groups that manage to keep 'veterans' as active members may be particularly effective in encouraging this.

It is less easy when examining this aspect of consumerism to draw firm conclusions on this role of self-help groups, or to give concrete examples. But they are most certainly important to enabling this strand of consumerism to develop. The question is, do professionals in fact all want this process to occur?

General Conclusions

Policy-makers need to consider the provision of services from the points of view of comprehensive cover and equity. One must doubt if services operated by self-help groups can meet these conditions. We must be realistic about their limitations and respect the wishes of some groups to have no involvement in this area. But where there is a real desire to do something, there may well be a case for developing services in partnership – as long as groups are not used as pawns in a cost-cutting game.

The second strand of consumerism, that of dialogue and comment, is one that could be most usefully developed, and could be helpful for both groups and those on the receiving end of their opinions. What is needed is general encouragement for groups and a range of opportunities for debate rather than necessarily a formal system of participation.

Personal involvement in the diagnosis and treatment of individual problems can be enhanced by more self-confidence. One can see the great potential for people who wish to join groups – and these are only a small minority of people with a problem – in personal development through membership. The contribution of self-help groups in this way is probably modest, but significant.

Implications for Professionals

How finally, could these trends be encouraged? In conclusion, let us consider ways in which professionals might change their practice to the benefit of themselves and individuals receiving their care.

First, to recap on the value of general support for self-help groups. Local resource centres, individual professional workers and national bodies can all enhance and back up the general work of groups by support, resources and money, and by increasing the flow of information about groups.

Secondly, professionals need to make time to learn about and understand groups. They can benefit from acquiring and reading literature, going to meetings, inviting groups to give talks and listening.

Thirdly, they need to accept the unpredictability and variety of groups. Involvement with them can be uncomfortable and challenging too, but they are not the ogres they might appear. An acceptance of the value of creative tension may help.

In practical terms, social work and other training could usefully include an examination of groups and professional attitudes to them, as is now done in Canada and elsewhere. Student placements have proved to be particularly valuable and could be developed relatively easily.

Finally, a more general point: self-help groups, as long as one is realistic about their contribution, must be considered seriously in an examination of consumerism. But it is not only such direct interaction, it is other opportunities social policy-makers and providers have to learn from them. Could not lessons be learnt from their strengths and put into practice, in the way services generally are planned and provided in the welfare state? It is here that their importance may well lie in the long run, rather than in the roles that have been outlined here.

References

Levy, L., 'Mutual Support Groups in Great Britain', in *Social Science and Medicine*, vol. 16 (1982), pp. 1265-75.

Parker, C. and Etherington, S., 'Time to get Street Wise', in *Social Work Today*, 13 May 1985, pp. 13-14.

Richardson, A. and Goodman, M., *Self-Help and Social Care: Mutual Aid Organisations in Practice*, PSI, 1983.

Unell, J., 'Nottingham Self-Help Groups Project: the First Year's Work', in Stephen Matel and Ilona Kickbusel (eds), *Self-Help and Health in Europe*, WHO, 1983.

Wilson, J., 'Support for Self Help', NCVO briefing, October 1983.

Wilson, J., 'Can You Kill it with Kindness?' *Voluntary Action*, July 1985.

12 Advocacy and Consumers: 'The Advocacy Alliance'
William Bingley

If one aspect of consumerism is about enabling people to make choices then not only should there be concern about the rights and services the consumer can actually choose from, but also how certain groups, particularly those who live in large institutions, can be assisted to make and implement those choices that have usually been regarded as not being their right or within their capacity. One reaction to this perceived powerlessness of certain consumers has been the concept of advocacy. The idea has been turned into reality in three long-stay mental handicap hospitals in south London by an organisation called Advocacy Alliance and this contribution looks at its experience.

Advocacy is a much-repeated word that is in danger of being debased by a multiplicity of usages. The *Oxford Dictionary* defines an advocate as 'one who pleads for another' and advocacy as 'the science or art of pleading causes'. This definition is insufficiently comprehensive or dynamic. Advocacy entails not only speaking on behalf of people but also seeking to promote the individual speaking on behalf of themselves. Advocacy is essentially about transferring some degree of personal power to people who, maybe because of their disability or where they live, are unable to influence to any significant degree the course of their lives or to claim rights to which they are entitled. The International League of Societies for Persons with Mental Handicap recognises three basic forms of advocacy.

1. *Self-advocacy*: This involves people with disabilities asserting their own rights, expressing their needs and assuming the duties of citizenship to the full extent of their capabilities.
2. *Legal advocacy*: A term used to describe the broad range of methods and activities by which lawyers and other legally trained individuals assist persons with disabilities to exercise and defend their rights. This can include reform or creation of new laws, as well as formal or informal activities to protect a citizen's rights or interests under existing law.
3. *Citizen advocacy*: Working on a one-to-one basis, unpaid trained volunteers who are independent of the service-givers, attempt to foster respect for the rights and dignity of persons with a disability and to ensure

that such people get at least an opportunity to enforce and obtain their rights.

One of the attractions of 'advocacy' is its universality of application: it can be relevant not only for people with disabilities but also those allegedly without. In this country the experience of advocacy has been confined to people with mental health problems or with a mental handicap. Twenty-eight mental illness hospitals now have some kind of legal advocacy project either resident in the hospital or periodically visiting the institution. Self-advocacy is being extensively promoted in both fields. Citizen advocacy is now established in London and Sheffield and other projects are being initiated. How has it worked? Advocacy Alliance has the longest experience of running a citizen advocacy project in this country and what follows is a description of its experiences.

What is Citizen Advocacy?

Citizen advocacy is well established in the USA and now has a statutory basis in the Developmentally Disabled Assistance and Bill of Rights Act. The concept is also well established in Sweden. In this country it is not so well developed, although the 1976 Review of the Mental Health Act (DHSS, 1976) recognised that 'the most important factor in safeguarding the position of a vulnerable patient and ensuring their rights are upheld is personal contact between the patient and somebody whose job it is to explain the position from the patient's point of view'. The concept of citizen advocacy owes much to Wolfensburger (1977), but in the context of Britain it has been defined by Sang (Sang, and O'Brien, 1984) as 'occurring when a private citizen enters into a relationship with and represents the interests of the mentally handicapped person who needs assistance to improve his or her quality of life and obtain full rights and entitlements by providing emotional support through friendship, spokespersonship, opportunities to learn new skills, and help in obtaining needed services. Volunteers work for the benefit and growth of people who are handicapped'. Three further aspects of citizen advocacy need to be emphasised.

1. The advocate is a volunteer. This is essential and highlights the fact that the relationship is based on friendship entered into freely on both sides. On the advocate's side, once he or she has paired with their partner, there is an expectation that the relationship will be long-term and part of the selection of advocates involves an assessment that they are able to realistically offer such a relationship.
2. The advocate must be competent. Training is essential not only to enable the advocate to communicate effectively with their partner and be sensitive to their needs but also to have an extensive knowledge of the various entitlements and choices that lay before their resident in any given circumstances.
3. The advocate must represent the interests of his or her partner as if they

were their own. This is an essential task for the advocate. They must develop a relationship where they can ascertain the interests of their partner. Frequently this will be easy because the resident will be able to express what he or she wants. Often, however, this will not be possible and the advocate will have to sensitively reach a conclusion as to what the resident's needs are and work towards their fulfilment.

The citizen advocate is more than a befriender. They must also be prepared where necessary not only to assist their partner to make choices but, equally important, to help them to implement those choices.

What is Advocacy Alliance?
Advocacy Alliance recruits and trains volunteers to be citizen advocates for residents in three south London long-stay mental handicap hospitals – St Ebba's Hospital, Epsom, Surrey; St Lawrence's Hospital, Caterham, Surrey and Normansfield Hospital, Teddington, Middlesex. It was launched in 1981 as a pilot project and is sponsored by five national voluntary organisations – MENCAP, One-to-One, MIND, The Spastics Society and The Leonard Cheshire Foundation. The Alliance is a private limited company that employs a Coordinator, an Administrative Assistant and also a Recruitment Officer who is currently funded through the DHSS Opportunities for Volunteering Scheme. Initial funding for the pilot project for three years has been provided by the DHSS with further contributions from the King's Fund Mental Health Foundation and other sources. The project is being independently evaluated. The pilot project stage, which has lasted longer than the envisaged three years, has now been concluded and it is hoped that in the long term the three existing projects will pass to local independent control, while the Alliance itself will continue as a resource and development office. The essential characteristics of the Advocacy Alliance and its workers is its independence of the service providers, a characteristic it shares with the citizen advocates themselves. It is important to grasp, however, that the central theme of the advocacy relationship is advocate loyalty. The citizen advocate's primary loyalty is to their partner and not to the advocacy programme, other residents, service-providing staff or anybody else. The job of those who actually work for Advocacy Alliance is primarily to facilitate their advocates and not to control them. This emphasis on the independent nature of citizen advocates is hard for people who are used to the hierarchical nature of voluntary and statutory agencies to understand (Sang, and O'Brien, 1984).

How were the Citizen Advocacy Projects Set Up?
A crucial difference in the legal framework of advocacy in this country and for instance the USA is that here there is no legal entitlement to an advocate. This meant, in relation to the three hospitals in which Advocacy Alliance is working, that the projects could only be set up with the agreement of the

hospital authorities and maybe more importantly that the projects remain active in the hospitals by agreement with those authorities. In 1981 negotiations were commenced immediately with St Ebba's and Normansfield and St Lawrence's Hospital came later. Not surprisingly, negotiations with the first two hospitals took considerably longer than those with the third. All three hospitals are different in size and characteristics and although negotiating agreements presented some common difficulties the process of initiating the projects was quite different in each hospital. In all three a crucial factor was support from key members of the staff and management. The process of establishing the projects had three important components.

1. *Negotiations*: Before any of the projects got under way full consultations were undertaken with the hospital management at divisional and district level, influential local groups such as Community Health Councils, Leagues of Friends and relevant voluntary organisations and with various staff and professional groups including local trade union officials. At the same time regular contact with the ward staff was initiated. The wards selected initially were those whose staff were interested and willing to cooperate. The project depended on a certain amount of 'built-in success' at the beginning and it was important to find the wards where the charge nurses/sisters were prepared to give up time and energy to a project which would inevitably provoke a great deal of curiosity and ambivalence on the part of many of their colleagues. At the outset the Alliance decided to concentrate their efforts on those areas of the hospital where there were residents who had no living friends or relatives or were not visited by anyone from the community. This identification was carried out in collaboration with the nursing and medical staff.

2. *Ethical code*: An important stage in the implementation of the project was the establishment of a working agreement with the hospitals. After extensive discussions an 'Ethical Code for Advocates' was agreed. This code lays down guidelines for both advocates and staff and its basis is the importance of the human rights and dignity of hospital residents (Advocacy Alliance, 1984).

3. *Project teams*: Project teams have been set up in each hospital to provide a means of monitoring the project. Membership of the team is composed of three people from Advocacy Alliance (the Coordinator together with two board members) and three people from the hospital (the hospital administrator, the voluntary services coordinator and the senior nursing officer). The team is usually chaired by the voluntary services organiser and any issue needing clarification or debate is reviewed at the team meetings.

The Advocates

Recruitment
Advocacy demands a long-term commitment and the ability to understand

and represent another person. The Alliance's recruitment material stresses two things: the nature/extent of the need for advocacy and the degree of commitment required. Because of the level of involvement, recruitment was limited by the need to find people who lived within easy reach of the hospital. Recruitment was undertaken by way of articles in the local press, leaflet distribution, leaflet and poster distribution to local groups, talks to local groups, public service announcements on both local TV and radio and also a TV programme made about the scheme.

Selection
Before becoming involved in the scheme the Coordinator must ascertain that the recruits are of the right temperament and that they understand and are capable of the degree of dedication that advocacy demands. The Alliance stipulates a minimum visiting requirement of two hours per week for an open-ended duration and looks for advocates who have a blend of concern and determination. A fairly high drop-out rate between recruitment and end of training is a phenomenon common to all training courses but it is undoubtedly higher in a project such as this. All candidates for the training courses are interviewed by the coordinator and are asked to complete a confidential interview sheet. Two references, one from an employer if applicable, are taken up. Recruits are also interviewed independently by the Voluntary Services Coordinator to ensure that they satisfy the hospital criteria for volunteers. Throughout the training period both the recruit and the Alliance assess each other and it is clearly established that at any time before the recruit is officially accepted as an advocate that both sides can indicate that the recruit's involvement in the scheme should end.

Training
Training of advocates is essential and has several functions. It helps to prepare trainees to become advocates, it enables them to meet residents and staff and it allows Alliance and hospital staff to assess the intent and commitment of trainees. The Alliance is continually developing its training programme but at present it consists of ten two-hour sessions and a one-day workshop over a ten-week period. It is done in the evenings and at weekends and covers such issues as the critical awareness of mental handicap, an introduction to the principles of normalisation, the role and function of the advocate and information about benefits and legal rights.

Identifying Residents Who Would Benefit from Advocacy
From the beginning of the scheme it was emphasised that all residents, regardless of age or degree of handicap, who had not been visited for a period of one year should be eligible for advocacy. Since the residents involved in the scheme are over the age of 18 parental consent is not necessary, although the Alliance contacts relatives (where they exist) to inform them of the possibility of an advocacy relationship and invite them to meet with the resident, trainee

advocate and Alliance staff. To date no difficulties have been experienced in this type of relationship.

The Matching Process
Throughout the training course trainees are encouraged to visit the hospitals as often as possible to meet eligible residents. Once a trainee has completed training and affirmed commitment the Coordinator, after consultation with the resident and the project team, confirms the advocacy relationship and informs all parties involved. The matching process is informal and no pressure is put on either side to pursue a relationship that is not satisfying to both of them. It is very difficult to describe how this process works but it has invariably resulted in a relationship forming between a citizen advocate and one particular resident.

Support
Once the relationship is established the advocate receives on-going support from other advocates, Alliance staff and the Alliance Board of Management. Support and advice are essential to ensure that advocates feel secure, particularly in matters of conflict with hospitals. The Support Group meetings, to which the advocates and trainees at each hospital are invited, are valuable and enable advocates to discuss their experiences and problems with each other and the Alliance Coordinator.

Complaints Procedure
The Coordinator is responsible for the general support of all advocates and in the case of any complaint against an advocate may ask the advocate to withdraw from the hospital until the matter is resolved. However, it is recognised that the hospital has the right to bar anyone who seriously abuses his or her position and all such cases should immediately be referred to a special meeting of the project team. Most matters of difficulty are resolved at ward level but if such resolution is not possible they should be referred to the appropriate Head of Department and then to the project team. The Alliance Board of Management reserves the right to raise in public debate any matters of policy arising from the work of advocates that it considers to be of significant importance to the rights of mentally handicapped people.

Insurance
The Alliance has public liability and personal accident insurance which covers advocates. This has been obtained through the NCVO (National Council for Voluntary Organisations).

Results
Four years after its birth Advocacy Alliance has 40 citizen advocates in the three hospitals. What assessments can be made of their impact on the lives of their partners (Sang, and O'Brien, 1984) distinguishes between instrumental

and expressive needs when discussing the role of the advocate. Fulfilment of instrumental needs enables people to receive goods, services and entitlement so as to lead a reasonable life and achieve full citizenship. Many of the advocates can illustrate success in this area. Advocates have been involved in medication issues, finding a more suitable location within the hospital and sorting out benefit entitlements. A number of the advocates are now actively involved in facilitating the movement of their residents outside the hospital. Coterminus with instrumental needs are expressive needs. Those who live in institutions are often starved of friendship, withdrawing from the social round that does not really exist. Advocates ameliorate that situation and are synthesising friendship and action in a way that no other volunteer and professional can do. The pilot projects have also revealed some problems. Recruitment has proved far harder than was originally envisaged. The reason for this is not because advocacy for mentally handicapped people is itself particularly daunting but because advocating for anybody requires a commitment that is extremely difficult for most people to make. Secondly, there is a difficulty, maybe more theoretical than real, about the authority of each advocate where their partner's disability is sufficient as to render them at least initially unable to indicate what they want. In reality there is almost nobody who cannot, once an advocacy relationship is well established, indicate some preference. The problem is really how the caring professionals regard the advocacy relationship. There is no legal relationship between advocates and partner. Apart from Mental Health Act guardianship, which is inappropriate, there is no adult guardianship in English law. Indeed, such a relationship would be an inappropriate model for advocacy. Essentially it is up to advocates to establish the legitimacy of their role in the eyes of the professionals and this calls for tact and a sense of diplomacy which at the same time does not involve inappropriate compromise.

Advocacy and Consumers

Initially at least individual advocacy in its widest sense obviously does not create a range of services and rights that do not already exist. For an individual it may result in a wider access to choice and entitlements that already exist but which have previously been denied because of an individual's inability to claim them unaided. As far as citizen advocacy is concerned, there will always be a limited supply of citizen advocates and therefore it must be seen as just one arrow in the quiver of advocacy methods. It is undoubtedly true however that advocacy, rooted in individual experience, can be the authority for organisations to propose and lobby for additional services and entitlement in the way, for example, that those voluntary organisations who sponsor Advocacy Alliance already undertake. Advocacy may also have a more subtle effect. Certainly within the mental health and mental handicap services advocacy has been prompted in part by the idea that promoting choice and accepting that people have rights has not been seen by many caring professionals as part of the objectives of the service. Too often care and rights are seen as mutually exclusive. Advocacy has the potential to change those assumptions.

References

Advocacy Alliance, *Guidelines for One-to-One Advocacy and Mental Handicap Hospitals*, 1984.

DHSS, *Review of the Mental Health Act 1959*, London, HMSO, 1976.

Sang, B. and O'Brien, J., *Advocacy. The UK and American Experience*. King's Fund Project Papers, 1984.

Wolfensburger, W. *A Balanced Multi-Component Advocacy Protection Scheme*, NIMR/CAMR Publications, Toronto, 1977.

13 Cooperatives and Consumerism: 'The Little Women Cooperative'
Nicholas Murray

Social work cooperatives are still in their infancy in Britain. Although the idea of cooperatives as a means of delivering certain welfare services has been well received there are still only two successfully established cooperatives currently functioning: the Little Women Household Services, an all-woman home help service in Sunderland, and Inter-Help Coop, a more client-oriented cooperative which enables elderly people with disabilities in the community in Derbyshire, in collaboration with able-bodied relatives and friends, to provide domiciliary care for each other, and thus avoid having to go into institutional care. There are, however, plans to launch cooperatives in other parts of the country like Newcastle, where the city's social services department is currently looking into the feasibility of some form of domiciliary care cooperative in the Gosforth area. A proposal in Kent to turn old people's homes into cooperatives ran into difficulties with local trade unions and, for a number of reasons, appears to have been shelved.

What this means is that there is a dearth of practical examples of social work cooperatives and a consequent shortage of convincing empirical evidence about the strengths and weaknesses of this form of service organisation, particularly in relation to the question of central concern here: do cooperatives give the consumer a better service than more conventional structures? Inevitably, the debate about the usefulness of cooperatives in social services has centred on the experience of Sunderland and on the more extensive experience of the Italian 'care worker' cooperatives in Bologna.

Many of the recent wave of cooperatives have made the pilgrimage to Bologna in northern Italy where the first of Italy's 300 care workers cooperatives – 'la Co-operativa Assistenza Domiciliare Infanzia Anziana e Infermi' (CADIAI) – was started ten years ago. A literal translation of the title is 'Cooperative for the provision of domiciliary care for the aged, the handicapped and the very young' but about 60 per cent of CADIAI's work is with the elderly. The cooperative's membership is about 80 people, 90 per cent of whom are women. Its main current contract is with the Bologna public health authorities to supply a specified number of 'care worker hours' annually until the end of 1986. The Italian cooperatives usually work under contract to a local authority, often in conjunction with its direct labour. They also perform certain functions which in this country would be the preserve of 'professionals' and consequently they enjoy a higher status than British home helps. One of the founder members of Little Women, Margaret Elliott, who has visited Bologna, has been quoted as saying: 'I'd like to see the status of home helps lifted.' She believes that a better job title could be found than 'home help' – for example, 'social care workers' – to reflect what is really done by these care workers. 'They do a lot more than scrubbing,' she has said (in Murray, 1985).

In Bologna the cooperative provides cleaning, cooking and shopping help, which is what the British home help does. But it also does the work of our care attendant in helping the elderly in and out of bed, bathing, feeding and help with the lavatory; some kinds of basic physiotherapy like exercising and keeping the limbs moving by walking along corridors; and some rehabilitation work that would be done here by an occupational therapist. Cooperative care workers also deal with bedsores and general health (our district nurses' role), and some of our social workers' tasks like advising on welfare rights, counselling, liaison with family and neighbours and increasing a client's 'social networks'. Their opinion will also be influential in assessing a client's needs and in deciding whether the client is in need of hospital care.

CADIAI had its origins in what could probably be described as the black economy when a group of home helps who had been working for private clients formed themselves into a cooperative in order to raise their professionalism and offer a higher standard of care. They then found work in a series of local authority contracts. Cooperative members work in mixed teams of five or seven, half of whom will be local authority employees, and the team co-ordinator is a local authority-trained social worker. Ultimately the local authority bears the responsibility. It is reported that members of CADIAI are not entirely happy with this local authority control and would prefer more autonomy.

The local authority regards the standard of service in Bologna as having risen as a result of the involvement of CADIAI, particularly in view of the high quality of training cooperative members have received, which has been of a higher quality in the past than the training given to the authority's direct labour and which has now been emulated by the Bologna authority.

CADIAI is managed by a president and vice-president, both trained social workers, backed up by an office staff of five, and all care workers are members of the cooperative. To become a member each worker must put down £85, 25 per cent on entry and the balance deducted from wages over the next six months. This is refunded if they leave. The cooperative's general meeting can choose whether to put profits into reserve or to distribute them as wage bonuses. It has a long waiting list of people wanting to join (Oakeshott, 1984).

Britain's pioneer home help cooperative, Little Women Household Services in Sunderland, appears to have more autonomy than the Bolognese venture. It was set up by a group of local working-class women who had already run a cooperative shop selling small portions of groceries for old people living on their own. After the shop project ended the women were looking for ideas for a new venture and the actual idea for a home help cooperative came from a development officer from Community Service Volunteers, Peter Smith.

The way in which Little Women was set up is instructive and shows the importance of laying the right foundations if certain pitfalls are to be avoided. One of these is getting on the right side of the trade unions. All ten women members of the cooperative are staunch members of NUPE and pay themselves the full trade union rate for the job. Right from the outset they talked to the unions to reassure them that they were not out to steal anybody's job. Fears that this was a form of privatisation, eating into local authority provision, were scotched right away. Margaret Elliott and her colleagues made clear that it was their intention to complement, not to substitute for, statutory services by providing home helps to people who would not be eligible for local authority social services department help anyway. Even now she is still worried that cooperatives may be seen as some form of back-door privatisation and get the cooperative idea a bad name: 'We don't want to be seen to be taking other people's jobs away.'

Little Women started meeting Sunderland social services department in the very early stages and talked to the head of the home help service and the organisers. The women obtained from the local authority statistics for the areas in which cooperative members lived and wanted to work and from these figures it was clear that the numbers of people in need of help far exceeded the numbers the local authority could cater for. Social services staff were very helpful and showed cooperative members in detail what duties were done by statutory home help employees, what their terms and conditions were, and even such things as how they filled out their record cards. In May 1983 the local authority pumped a large amount of money into its home help service increasing provision by 25 per cent. Although this possibly delayed the start of Little Women by meeting some of the demand they wanted to address, it was a significant factor in reassuring the doubters that Little Women was not expanding at the expense of the local authority provision.

Little Women also had meetings with councillors to ensure that they had political backing for collaboration with social services in referring clients whom the department couldn't help. They also wanted to stress to the elected members that they were bringing central government money into the town that the local authority couldn't get and that with this money came employment. As Margaret Elliott (Elliott and Smith, 1985) explains in her account of the setting up of Little Women:

> We told councillors that we were a third sector – not public or private – and that we held ourselves accountable not only to our clients but to the trade unions and the local authority. We did this by having a facility in our constitution which enabled a representative from the client group, the local authority and from the trade unions to sit on our committee. They would be there to listen and advise.

After meeting the councillors, Elliott and her colleagues took their arguments to the trade unions who, while not wholehearted in their support, were certainly not opposed to the cooperative:

> We stressed that we were a democratic organisation owned and controlled by the members and that we were mindful of our social objectives as well as our practical ones. Social objectives being to provide a caring and useful operation where clients as well as workers had a say in the quality of the service. The workers being mindful that the whole community is part of us, as we are of it. The practical side being that we were creating jobs, real and lasting jobs and with that comes the spin-off of regenerating the local economy.

Little Women is financed quite straightforwardly from payments by clients (although an initial urban aid grant of £3000 saw the venture off the ground). Clients who are supplementary benefit claimants can receive a special needs allowance from the DHSS to pay for home help services at the rate of £2.40 per hour. An agreement was reached between the local DHSS and Little Women that they would notify the cooperatives of clients whom Little Women felt needed home help. The client would then be visited by the DHSS, their eligibility assessed and a number of hours a week agreed. Private clients who do not receive DHSS help pay £2.50 an hour, a fee in many cases paid by relatives. The women themselves are paid the same rate of £2 an hour as local authority home helps (currently under review to rise by ten pence to £2.10 per hour). About 80 per cent of clients are paid for by the DHSS which symbolises the dependency of this non-statutory initiative on the statutory sector. Indeed, the recent government proposals to review the social security system created a fear in the summer of 1985 that special needs allowances might be abolished and the foundation of Little Women's efforts be kicked away from under them.

If that storm can be weathered, Little Women intend looking at the possibility of expanding into services for carers of elderly relatives, possibly relieving them for periods on a regular basis. This would be a respite service for carers – 'granny sitting' – which the local authority does not at present provide.

Social work cooperatives like Little Women are obviously here to stay but is there any substance in the charge, which the Sunderland project has been most careful to rebut, that cooperatives are privatisation under another name? Robert Oakeshott of Job Ownership Limited, which arranged the trip to Bologna for Margaret Elliott and Anne Charlton, who is carrying out the Newcastle feasibility study, which published the results of that visit, and which exists to promote 'worker-owned businesses', prefers to talk of 'de-municipalisation'. He believes that local authority services do not give value for money, job satisfaction or consumer satisfaction, and that transfer of these services to employee-owned businesses is a desirable goal. He has advised Kent on its aborted plans to look at 'alternative management' of old people's homes. Although there are obvious correspondences between these views and those of the privatisation lobby, Robert Oakeshott insists that 'we are not advocates of reverting to a simple capitalist arrangement'. His publicity material states that: 'The key definition of a job-ownership company is that it is in principle owned and controlled by the people working in it and only by them'. This could be a definition of socialism or it could be a description of a successful capitalist organisation where there is exclusive profit-sharing by employees.

Some of the worries about privatisation, such as poor working conditions and rates of pay, would not apply – presumably – to employee ownership where employees would have no interest in voting to exploit themselves. But is there any guarantee that people *outside* the cooperative – clients – couldn't be exploited by an unscrupulous cooperative? This would seem to be a fairly fundamental question to be answered. On the face of it, a social work cooperative provides new services that the local authority could not provide if it is like Little Women, or provides existing services in a better way – if you accept the now familiar indictment of statutory services as remote, bureaucratic, inflexible and unresponsive to consumers. Certainly, the consumers of home help services in Sunderland will, on all the available evidence, have cause to be grateful to Little Women. A small, happy, caring group of people who work better because they work for themselves and who are freed from cumbersome red tape or the disabling cynicism which can afflict employees of large bureaucratic organisations, must surely be giving clients a better service.

But what if a 'bad' cooperative set up, which didn't have high ideals and which simply wanted to make money for its members with little regard for the quality of care it gave? Is there anything in the cooperative structure which *necessarily* makes its service better *for those who are not its members*? That is a question that has to be answered fairly directly if social work cooperatives are to be hailed unambiguously as the way forward for better, consumer-satisfying services. This inevitably brings us on to the question of accountability.

Almost by definition a cooperative is answerable only to itself ('controlled by the people working in it and only by them' – Robert Oakeshott) and its constituent members. A self help cooperative – like the Derbyshire group Inter-Help – where members and clients are one and the same people should be able to avoid what Little Women avoids by sheer good faith and commitment to its caring goals. Consumer control of a welfare cooperative can only be ensured in a totally satisfying way if consumers, clients, are part of it, otherwise they have no way of exercising influence on it other than by exercising the final right of the consumer of a service in the market-place: to decline to pay for it. But do consumers of social services always have that choice?

There is another kind of accountability, too – public accountability. At present a statutory social services authority has no right of inspection of a service provided by a cooperative unless the area of operation – an old people's home for example where there is a requirement to register with the local authority – is covered by legislation. If there were to be a mushroom growth of social work cooperatives this might become a serious issue for the responsible authorities to confront.

The ultimate brake on any rapid acceleration of cooperatives might be the nature of social work provision itself. Who would be anxious to set up a child abuse cooperative, for example? Some services clearly lend themselves to this form of organisation more than others. The conspicuous success of Little Women has much to do with the fact that it operates at local level and has an optimum size which is small and local. It is unlikely that there would be a rush to establish a cooperative for dealing with difficult, demanding client groups where the financial return, or investment, might be much more problematic. Nevertheless, if social work cooperatives in the future are to be as scrupulous and committed as Little Women consumers of their services will have little cause for concern.

References

Elliott, M. and Smith, P., 'How to start a Home Cooperative', Community Service Volunteers, London, 1985.
Murray, N., 'Owning Your Own Job', *Community Care*, 31 January 1985.
Oakeshott, R., *Cooperative Social Work in Bologna*, Job Ownership Ltd., London, 1984.

14 Consumer Participation and Management: 'The Liverpool Parent Governor Support Project'
Joan Evans

Liverpool was one of the first local authorities to involve parents on school governing bodies, well before it became a legal requirement. Yet until recently little help has been available to assist them in actually undertaking such a task. This chapter describes a project specifically designed to enable parent governors to participate in the management of their schools.

In the early 1980s some people involved in Liverpool Association of Parents Concerned with Education (LASPA), a local pressure group, recognised this issue and resolved to do something about this situation. Parent governors they had been in contact with felt they would benefit from meeting their counterparts from other schools, in addition to wanting more information. The group of LASPA members and others who became involved successfully approached the Joseph Rowntree Trust for funding for a part-time worker for two years to work on Parent Governor Support Services. The worker's brief was to contact every parent governor in the area and also the schools, the LEA and appropriate community groups. The aim was to enable parent governors to work more effectively, ensure that the parental voice was heard within the education system and improve parent governors' self-image. Its wider brief was to assist parents to realise their responsibilities for the style of their children's schools.

The project worker commenced in September 1982. Although she was successful in contacting a number of parent governors and publicising the scheme, problems occurred because of a lack of a recognised work-base. Notwithstanding a variety of parent governors' concerns were identified and a Handbook for parent governors was produced, which supplied the new parent governor with all the basic information he or she would require.

In addition, links were forged with the LEA officers. The Director of Education was very interested in the project and initiated meetings with parent governors, the results of which were fed back to the LEA. He was involved in the discussions which led to the formation of a Parent Governor Support Project (PGSP) under the auspices of a community programme (MSC).

A key feature of the scheme was a staff training programme drawn up by the Workers Educational Association (WEA). The programme was for three weeks and aimed to help the workers to familiarise themselves with the education system, with particular reference to Liverpool; to gain awareness of the problems facing parent governors; how committee meetings work and how a parent governor can best function at such meetings. Meetings were arranged with head teachers, teachers, parent governors and parents and they visited parent school partnership rooms in local schools. (These are drop-in centres for parents and toddlers where further education and leisure interest classes for parents are held while the children are looked after.) A major aim of the training was to draw parallels between the process the outreach workers were going through, increasing their confidence and self-motivation with that of parent governors' experience, which we aimed to help them with. In addition to this comprehensive training programme, on-the-job training was necessary as issues arose. It was apparent that most of the workers needed some time to build up their confidence to help them deal easily with meetings. They also needed to have detailed factual information available for putative parent governors. It was necessary therefore continuously to update the stock of information that the project as a whole held, so we could respond promptly to queries from parent governors brought in by outreach workers.

The basic aims of the project were to give parent governors the support and advice they required through the appointment of 'outreach workers'. This would involve workers establishing contact with parent governors in their areas and attempting to set up self-help group networks, involving all interested parties, including retired parent governors to benefit from their experiences. Another important objective was to produce written information; a regular newsletter and packages of factual information, which could be regularly updated, to help parent governors do their job. The project was also to offer clerical support to parent governors (an offer which was not taken up to any real extent).

It was considered essential to involve parent governors and encourage them to initiate meetings etc., rather than workers doing it themselves. It was also essential that the project was not seen to be controversial before it had achieved some positive results. This was particularly important given the project's stated aim to establish a regular structure for communicating with the LEA, as the only way of ensuring things really changed.

Each small area team of outreach workers was assigned a sector of the city to work in. The outreach teams were encouraged to get to know their areas, investigate community organisations, of which we had details in the office, find out about the people in their communities – what motivated them to go to meetings, what their concerns were and to hear alternative views of the schools in the area from community workers and activists.

Teams approached their work in different ways; some felt it was very important to have a local base which they believed parent governors would come to when they needed help. These teams advertised weekly workshops at their local base using a newsletter but these were not very successful except when tacked onto the end of a parent's group bingo session. This may have been because parent governors did not feel their problem was severe enough to take up such a workshop, or they were unwilling to attend unless something specific was on offer. In a sense, workers may have been too available without giving anyone the incentive to attend.

Initially, workers made contact directly to schools with the head teacher. There were some initial problems associated with this in that heads were suspicious of the project. However, as publicity about the scheme increased and information put out by the project was distributed, this ceased to be a problem.

Workers also communicated directly with parent governors using a newsletter and inviting them to attend meetings. In addition, all parents in Liverpool were given details of the project in a letter sent out by the LEA inviting parents to stand for parent governor, or to nominate a friend.

Some workers were more successful than others at becoming established in their areas and developing a full range of contacts and informing them about PGSP. This resulted from the differing levels of experience, confidence and enthusiasm that workers possessed and also the degree of community activity in the area. However, they were all effective in communicating with Parent Governors assisting them in raising issues of concern and resolving their specific problems.

Meetings with and visits to staff from some of the many different branches of the LEA structure were set up. These included a youth liaison tutor, education welfare officers, an educational psychologist, teachers, headmasters, the officer from the LEA office responsible for school governors and the officer responsible for special education. Education welfare officers were particularly interested in having regular meetings with PGSP workers in order to have feedback from parent governors and parents. They were keen to know parents' anxieties about schools as they recognised the benefits of parental support for their children's schools.

Another interesting development was in a Roman Catholic primary school in Liverpool 8, with a high percentage of ethnic minority children; and through this, Catholic Social Services social workers who were working with the school's staff to involve parents in the parent governor elections – the first for church schools. This school held a series of meetings, backed up with impressive publicity handouts, with bold graphics and clearly written text, which were sent to all parents. These meetings were well attended and resulted in eight nominations for the two parent governor openings.

The pioneer project had already identified many parent governor needs and the main project unearthed additional areas. These can be categorised under the broad headings of:

1. Information flow to parent governors.
2. The legal limitations and requirements of the role of parent governor and the other governors.

3. Communicating with and involving the rest of the parents.

The sort of information parent governors wanted to know was often on health and safety matters, whom to contact in the LEA office over these matters, how elections should be run, alternative reading schemes, what could be done about racism in schools. The racism issue was raised with the LEA and a copy of their multicultural education policy was forwarded to all parent governors. The project encouraged all parent governors to have it discussed as an agenda item at governors' meetings. Further the project ensured that parent governors were kept informed of policy changes, e.g. changes to discipline and suspension procedures, new initiatives in special schools etc., and the services that the LEA had to offer such as education welfare, education guidance, speech therapy, etc.

On the legal side, many prospective and new parent governors wanted to know what their obligations were and what it was possible for them to do. There was also uncertainty as to what the parent governor's role was with regard to staff appointments. It was apparent that parent governors had been made to feel like second-class governors and other governors had done little to alleviate this. Parent governors also wanted to know who the other governors were and their roles and function.

The issue of communicating with parents, interesting and involving them, was seen as crucial. Parent governors were anxious about getting publicity to parents, being assured access to them in the school setting or elsewhere, if parents preferred. The best method of ensuring parents came to meetings was a subject of discussion with parent governors and schools and it was apparent there was no easy answer, but the example of the Roman Catholic school referred to earlier showed it could be done. The new community schools in Liverpool have 'parent Coordinators' whose responsibility is to ensure that there is communication between the school and parents. It is envisaged that parent governors will work closely with parent Coordinators and PGSP outreach workers have made contact with them regarding this and to involve the feeder primary schools before intake.

PGSP produced written information, aimed at both existing and prospective parent governors. A newsletter was regularly produced which included articles on policy changes and issues taken up by parent governors and also details of workshops and conferences of interest to parent governors. The presentation of this paper was fairly light-hearted and included graphics and poems as well as more weighty items. More details of the legislation covering parent governors were included in the 'Election Pack', which is a collection of papers drawn up by PGSP workers and presented in clear and easily understandable text with cartoon-type illustrations. Another aim of this particular package was to help the chairs of governing bodies and heads to be aware of the parent governors' role and their concerns and what needs to be considered when running an election. These were distributed to all county primary schools by the LEA and proved extremely popular.

The second task was the development of an 'Information Pack' which was to include information on a number of different topics ranging from health and safety in schools, social education, pastoral care, discipline, curriculum development to parental participation. This pack would not be specific to Liverpool and could be used more widely.

A successful Open Day/Election Workshop was held in 1985 prior to elections to offer support to prospective parent governors. It was also suggested that PGSP should act as an 'ideas exchange', sharing knowledge and experience gained. This would be achieved through gathering information from national and international organisations on matters of interest to parent governors and parents to enable PGSP to compare and contrast situations. It would also collate information and experiences from all over the city, which could be fed back to the LEA and national organisations.

To conclude, I would like to identify some issues which relate to the effectiveness of the project, in addition to the specific points already raised. To summarise, these points are to do with the staff's role, and status, relationships with the Management Committee and communication with the LEA.

First, some of the workers had problems about their role. Sometimes, problems occurred with heads who seemed to see the worker as an imposition, not as a professional who had legitimate reasons for contacting the school.

It was necessary for workers (and those they were dealing with) to see themselves as a link between clients and professionals in the education system. Yet because the scheme was funded by the MSC the workers were often inexperienced. This was exacerbated by the job being part-time, low-paid and temporary (one year). This is a common feature of MSC-funded projects.

The fact that the jobs were part-time (apart from the two supervisory posts) had another effect in that there were two aspects to the work: first, that of working out in the field on a face-to-face basis; and secondly, that of undertaking research to keep up the stock of information PGSP required to keep pace with parent governors' queries. The demand for information and help in solving problems was exceptionally heavy. It would therefore have been advantageous to have had full-time workers who had responsibility for research and building up useful contacts with the LEA in particular. Furthermore, parent governors in Liverpool are now elected for a three-year period, so it is not really helpful to have support workers who are in post for just one year as this means all relationships having to be re-established annually.

The final area of concern is that of liaison with the LEA. It is important that channels of communication are well established. It is evident in Liverpool that the will to involve parents exists in that there have been parent governors for ten years. The Parent School Partnership exists for this purpose and now the parent Coordinators in community schools are there specifically to communicate with parents and there has been a good deal of cooperation from the LEA. It is the nitty-gritty business of making this really effective which needs working on. The recent political climate in Liverpool has detracted from new initiatives as job security has taken precedence in people's minds.

Hopefully this wouldn't be a problem elsewhere and various means of communicating with parents could be tried out in cooperation with the LEA.

Index